Management for Professionals

More information about this series at http://www.springer.com/series/10101

Nils Urbach • Frederik Ahlemann

IT Management
in the Digital Age

A Roadmap for the IT Department
of the Future

 Springer

Nils Urbach
University of Bayreuth
Bayreuth, Germany

Frederik Ahlemann
University of Duisburg-Essen
Essen, Germany

ISSN 2192-8096   ISSN 2192-810X   (electronic)
Management for Professionals
ISBN 978-3-319-96186-6   ISBN 978-3-319-96187-3   (eBook)
https://doi.org/10.1007/978-3-319-96187-3

Library of Congress Control Number: 2018951417

This Springer imprint is published by the registered company Springer Nature Switzerland AG
The registered company address is: Gewerbestrasse 11, 6330 Cham, Switzerland

Testimonials

Digitalization has far-reaching consequences for today's companies. It is not only an option anymore, but a necessity—especially for their IT departments. This book shows what IT managers need to be prepared for. Particularly worth reading.

Markus Bentele
Vice President Information Technology/Group CIO, MAHLE International GmbH

A compulsory read for CEOs and CIOs alike. This book illustrates the strategic and entrepreneurial importance of IT in an excellent and easily digestible way. CIOs receive very good support in focusing on the important and relevant topics of IT transformation. Enjoy reading and implementing.

Bernhard Koch
Vice Chairman of the Executive Board, GFFT e.V.

This book demonstrates the impact of digital transformation on IT organizations and their management. It also presents potential risks for technology availability, security, and data protection. The authors develop a vision of what IT management should look like in 10 years if it is to continue playing an important role in the company. The book seeks to motivate IT executives and managers with IT responsibility to actively adapt their thinking and their IT organizations before they are forced to react to external pressure. Definitely worth reading!

Sven Kreimendahl
Director Business Technology Services, Campana & Schott

The book gives a comprehensive and well-positioned overview of the various facets of digitalization. With the presented hypotheses and their direct formulation, the authors polarize very strongly, whereby the reader himself compares the old with the new world and is forced to take a stand. As the responsible person in the IT area, it is difficult to evade this. This book is suitable for both commencing with and reflecting on own digitalization initiatives, and I recommend that it should be read urgently!

Dr. Benedikt Martens
Senior Project Manager, Evonik Industries AG

The partially radical hypotheses address the current and future challenges of IT in a corporate group extremely accurately. With the future "innovate-design-transform" model, the authors describe modern collaboration models of IT and business, together with innovative partnerships, in a comprehensible and practice-relevant way.

Dr. Kian Mossanen
Chief Information Officer, DRÄXLMAIER Group

For me, digitalization means automation and new business models. IT departments were always involved with automation, but new business models are partly an existential challenge for companies and their IT departments. This book comprehensively shows what this entails for today's IT departments and managers.

Michael Neff
Former CIO, RWE AG

In times of rapid—also technological—changes, agility is required. That is why IT must be restructured within the company and why old paradigms must be abandoned. In their book, the authors impressively show what needs to be considered. From my point of view, a must read for CIOs, but also for CEOs and CDOs.

Burkhard Schütte
Retired Partner and Former Chief Information Officer, PricewaterhouseCoopers AG

Driven by digitalization, IT departments will undergo significant change in the coming years. This book shows in which direction the journey is heading. Recommended reading for everyone who is responsible for IT in companies or who wants to prepare for digitalization.

Dr. Roland Schütz
Chief Information Officer, Deutsche Lufthansa AG

The book provides informative insights into IT management in times of digitalization. On the basis of ten hypotheses, the two authors take a differentiated look at digital transformation and show which changes are associated with this process in the company. The recommendations derived from this give IT managers helpful suggestions for a technically sound discussion of the topic.

Thomas Ullrich
Board Member, DZ BANK AG

Foreword

Digital transformation is the megatrend of our time, heatedly discussed not just in Germany but all around the world. After all, it brings countless changes with it and as many new challenges as opportunities. That might not sound especially sensational at first. After all, corporate IT departments have dealt with constant change for years—not only new applications and technologies, but even comprehensive approaches like outsourcing and cloud computing. One major difference to earlier developments stands out, however; the digital revolution is arising from many new technologies at once, among them big data analytics, social media, cognitive services, mobile computing, the Internet of Things, artificial intelligence, and virtual and augmented reality—to only name a few of the most important.

For companies, this means carrying out countless projects for development, innovation, and strategy—all despite often only having a vague idea of the end goal. The way forward is often unclear. That overwhelms most traditional IT departments. They are accustomed to drawing up plans from requirements management and providing specialist departments with changes according to detailed release plans and the waterfall method. But that does not cut it anymore. The future of IT will only function with the necessary efficiency when its commodity services are highly standardized—such as with electric sockets. Just as energy providers supply electricity, standardized interfaces from cloud providers will offer what we still call "office IT." What once was "owned" will soon be simply "used." The future certainly still has room for improvement. We can imagine, for instance, a kind of IT stock exchange for commodity services.

Even today, in fact, companies with their own development department for standardized platforms and IT services have practically dwindled from existence. Outsourcing may increase efficiency, but it has yet to exhaust its competitive advantages. Standardized platforms and cloud services—like electricity—could be used by many other companies at once. IT departments must expand their scope from merely increasing their productivity and actively participate in value creation. What would that look like? We are beginning to realize that actual added value can be created by linking previously separate information and connecting multiple technologies. This is where IT management must place its center of gravity in the age of digitalization. IT must employ comprehensive big data analyses to work with company management and specialist departments to question existing business models and allow new technologies to continue developing or even restructure them.

IT management should be internally structured to increase production and creativity, enabling innovation through agile methods. It should be integrated into departments and encourage new business models and markets. That includes innovations for higher added value, new opportunities in marketing and sales, creating new communication channels, and shaping the workplace of the future. This also leads to an increase in employee satisfaction. Customer experience management must also be established to actively point the way from a satisfied customer to a brand ambassador. This indicates just how involved IT departments are in value creation. They are responsible for arming and fortifying staff against competition. They also expand their customer bases to other market segments for more growth and business activities.

All told, digital transformation certainly has disruptive consequences for many companies and industries. But continuing analog business is no longer an option. Technological innovation is already an important competitive factor for business today, with a significant influence on products, services, business processes, and sales and supply channels.

This book demonstrates the significant impact of digitalization on IT organizations and their management, as well as the risks to overcome, especially for technology availability, security, and data protection. The authors provide answers to many questions and explain what IT management should look like in 10 years if it is to continue playing an important role in the company. Their book seeks to motivate IT executives and managers with IT responsibility to actively adapt their thinking and their IT organizations before they are forced to react to external pressure. If it gets to that point, it might already be too late.

Director Business Technology Services,   Sven Kreimendahl
Campana & Schott
Cologne, Germany
April 2018

Preface

The digitalization topic has become an integral part of political debate, economic news, as well as internal company projects and coordination. Keywords such as *big data, cloud computing, digital transformation, Industry 4.0*, and *Internet of things* constantly arise in public and internal company discussions. There are, however, still many questions that remain unanswered, such as the implications of digitalization for individual industries, as well as the impact thereof, which IT departments in companies will have to consider in future. Today's IT bosses would usually like to claim the topic for themselves. This is not unexpected, because their departments are responsible for information technology in companies, and digitalization promises to expand their sphere of activity, or at least to strengthen their role.

However, many CIOs and IT executives encounter problems. Their IT departments are often seen as pure service providers with no particular innovation skills. Business customers—that is, the other departments in their own company—often act independently of the IT department when developing IT-based business and process innovations. An example of this is a marketing department that starts big data initiatives without involving the in-house technology experts. Such a situation is not surprising, since IT department employees are still very technology oriented and often have little or no business know-how. Furthermore, creativity, entrepreneurship, and innovation activities often have merely a shadow existence in an industrialized IT department, which is focused on reliability and stability. Most IT departments are structurally and procedurally not prepared to play a special role in digital transformation. For example, they lack functioning innovation management processes or effective technology scouting. Past cost optimizations also contribute to this: their capacities are rarely sufficient to test and implement new ideas beyond daily business. Consequently, IT managers feel uncertain: How can we position ourselves in this situation? How should we approach digital transformation? Where do we begin? What role will we play in future?

This book identifies these questions and intends to answer them from a specific perspective. It illustrates the digitalization implications for today's IT departments—with their structures, processes, and people. In particular, this book discusses the meaning of digitalization, it presents a picture of corporate IT in 10–15 years' time, and it illustrates how current managers can prepare for this development.

The target groups of this book are IT executives (e.g., CIOs, IT managers), managers who are also responsible for IT (e.g., CFOs), and academics with practical interests. This book intends to help not only with responding to the digital transformation, but also with playing an active role in order to proactively manage the fate of the IT department. Our concept of the future IT department is not cast in stone but should rather be understood as a sound basis for discussions and projections. Although not all the hypotheses in this book apply equally to all companies and industries, they will enable the development of individual future scenarios that can serve as a basis for your strategic planning and decision making.

This is not a scientific book—it does not meet the strict scientific requirements of a theoretical basis or empirical analysis. Our thoughts and insights are instead based on exploratory research, conversations and interviews with executives, the observation of technological developments, and the interpretation of the aforementioned sources. Where scientific knowledge was available, we naturally integrated it.

We hope you enjoy this book and invite all readers to enter into a dialog with us. Please feel free to contact us for questions, discussions, and suggestions.

Bayreuth, Germany   Nils Urbach
Essen, Germany   Frederik Ahlemann
April 2018

Contents

About the Authors

Prof. Dr. Nils Urbach is Professor of Business Informatics and Strategic IT Management at the University of Bayreuth. In addition, he is Deputy Director of the Finance & Information Management (FIM) Research Center and the Project Group Business and Information Systems Engineering of Fraunhofer FIT. Nils Urbach has been working in the fields of strategic information management and collaborative information systems for several years. In his current research, he focuses on digital transformation, smart devices, and blockchain, among others.

Nils Urbach studied information systems at the University of Paderborn and received his doctorate from EBS Business School, Wiesbaden, Germany. He gained international experience during his research stays at the University of Pittsburgh and the Université de Lausanne. He also worked for several years as a management consultant for Accenture and for Horváth & Partners in Frankfurt, Germany. His research results have been published in international journals and conference proceedings. Nils Urbach advises several companies on strategic IT management issues and regularly speaks on this topic.

Prof. Dr. Frederik Ahlemann holds the chair of Information Systems and Strategic IT Management at the University of Duisburg-Essen. In addition, he is the executive director of the Institute of Computer Science and Business Informatics at this university, and he is managing an international network of universities for the exchange of information systems students. His research topics include digital transformation, digital business strategies, enterprise architecture management, as well as project and project portfolio management. He also teaches these topics at university and as further training courses with experts and managers. Research questions are always examined from a practice-oriented and behavioral scientific perspective.

Frederik Ahlemann studied information systems at the University of Münster, Germany, and subsequently worked as a consultant in the area of project portfolio management. In 2006, he got his doctorate at the University of Osnabrück, Germany, and headed the Competence Center for Strategic IT Management at the EBS Business School, Wiesbaden, Germany, from 2006 to 2012. In 2010, he was a guest researcher at the University of South Florida, Tampa, USA. He is the author of a large number of specialist publications and works in research, as well as practice, and has collaborated with a number of companies from the automotive, financial services, energy, mechanical engineering, consulting, and IT sectors. As a speaker, he regularly gives lectures on the mentioned topics at national and international conferences.

The Digital Revolution: How Technological Trends Change the Business World

At present, the business world is changing drastically. Applying and using new information technologies in the business context lead to a significant change. In certain cases, it can even lead to the displacement of established business and value chain models—and this at an enormous speed. British journalist, Hamish McRae, exemplifies this change with the companies Uber, Facebook, Alibaba, and Airbnb. These four companies can be regarded as purely digital companies, since their Internet-based business models are fundamentally based on the innovative use of modern information technologies. All four companies are also market leaders in their respective segments and have replaced established competitors in a relatively short period of time. A closer look reveals to what extent the new, successful market players differ from their competitors who have "traditional" business models. Uber is, for instance, probably the largest taxi company in the world, but does not own a single taxi. The world's most popular media company, Facebook, does not produce its own content. Alibaba, the world's largest retailer, maintains no warehouse stock levels. And Airbnb, the world's largest provider of accommodation, does not own hotels. Hamish McRae summarizes the development as follows: "Something big is going on" [1]. In addition to the intensity of these developments, the speed of transformation is remarkable. A central reason for this is the changed speed at which users accept new media at the consumer level. While radio took 38 years and television 13 years to gain an audience of 50 million people, the Internet's "conquest" took only 3 years. Recent Internet-based services such as Facebook, Twitter, and Instagram took less than 12 months [2].

Consumers generally receive the described developments quite positively, because these often lead to noticeable advantages such as greater convenience, faster purchase transactions, or lower prices—although they also lead to a loss of privacy and data protection. Companies have more mixed feelings about this change. On the one hand, digital business model and value creation innovations give particularly small, start-up companies an opportunity to use good ideas to enter not only new, but also traditional markets with new products and services. On the other hand,

© Springer International Publishing AG, part of Springer Nature 2019
N. Urbach, F. Ahlemann, *IT Management in the Digital Age*, Management for Professionals, https://doi.org/10.1007/978-3-319-96187-3_1

established corporations particularly face an increasing risk of falling victim to the so-called disruptive effects of the new business world. The commercial use of information technology is, therefore, significantly boosted in many companies under the buzzword of "digitalization." While corporate IT has been heavily industrialized over the past few years—that is, especially streamlined for efficiency—numerous digitalization initiatives are at present characterizing the project landscape of many large corporations.

New Technologies Change Business

The technological achievements of recent years can be viewed as the trigger for the current "digital revolution." According to the study results of Accenture and Oxford Economics, digital technologies can contribute USD 1.36 trillion to the overall global economic performance by 2020 [3]. In the following, we shall present selected technological innovations which, from our point of view, are particularly important for the current change in the corporate world. Interestingly, almost none of these developments are groundbreaking innovations; they are usually further developments of existing, partly-established technologies and approaches, which have reached the necessary maturity and can be combined in such a way that they can generate significant business benefits.

A central technological innovation is the improved capability of processing huge amounts of data in a very short time. This is one of the major, recent "hot topics" in the IT world and is still being discussed under the keywords *big data analytics* or *smart data analytics*. The current techniques differ from the earlier "business intelligence" approaches in that really large amounts of data can be processed efficiently. A special feature of the new approaches is that standardized data capturing is not a strict prerequisite for its processing. Algorithms and approaches for text recognition or the analysis of real-time audio, as well as video streams, are also part of the *big data* approach. The development of ever more powerful processors and new memory technologies, such as in-memory databases and special analysis methods, have now made the decisive breakthrough possible. The analysis of mass data, which could not be achieved with conventional data analysis methods, has now become the innovation driver of many companies. ThyssenKrupp Elevator's intelligent elevator is a vivid example of an innovative big data application. A new elevator monitoring system, developed jointly with Microsoft and CGI, gives technicians access to real-time data to define a necessary repair before a breakdown occurs (predictive maintenance). Earlier approaches only allowed a response to an error alarm. Another example is the predictive analytics approach at Kaiser's Tengelmann to automate merchandise and sales planning. Blue Yonder's big data solution enables automatic, data-based orders of goods for selected assortments. This prevents costly stock shortages and leads to easier and cheaper merchandise planning for the respective branch [4].

Another technological innovation is the focus on the organizational use of social media. As a rule, we understand social media as Internet-based software systems that allow their users to network and exchange information with each other. Usually, this also includes the possibility of sharing or creating multimedia content. In contrast to times when technological innovations were first introduced in companies before they were subjected to mass consumer use, social media worked the other way around—a central feature of so-called IT consumerization [5]. For example, at a relatively early stage, end users began using weblogs as journalistic platforms, wikis as a platform for encyclopedias, or online social networks for networking with business or private contacts. A key characteristic of these services (such as Facebook, YouTube, Wikipedia) is that the users act as content providers and consumers at the same time. In essence, the providers merely provide a platform and, at best, carry out the necessary moderation and control functions. The rapidly increasing popularity of social media coupled with rapid growth rates, has changed the way in which people use the Internet and media in general—especially among younger users—to such an extent that the social media topic, although delayed, appeared on the agenda of certain corporate strategists. Since then, social media have increasingly been used for internal and external purposes. New channels for marketing, sales, and service processes such as Facebook, Twitter, WhatsApp, or Skype are presently being used for external communication, especially at the customer interface. For internal purposes, specific solutions are used to support organizational knowledge management (e.g., Microsoft Yammer or IBM Connect).

Cloud computing is yet another major "hot topic" of recent years. In our view, it actually triggered a paradigm shift in the provision of IT infrastructures and can therefore be regarded as a major driver of the digital revolution. The core idea of cloud computing is that IT services (e.g., storage, software, infrastructure) can be abstracted from the details of their physical nature and made available, or used, through a network (usually the Internet). This abstraction leads to the fact that it is no longer necessary or decisive for the consumer—at least in the form of the public cloud—to know where the infrastructure is located and how it is provided ("IT services from the cloud"). Although cloud computing's main technological innovation is the efficient use of virtualization technologies and increased network bandwidths, cloud computing brought us very close to the vision of "IT from the wall socket." Cloud computing, similar to social media, initially found widespread use in the private context. Examples of prominent services that reached high double-digit million user numbers in a very short period of time include Dropbox, Apple iCloud, Google Docs, and Microsoft Office 365. Although the concept is not entirely new in the business context (salesforce.com and its CRM system have been on the market since 1999), cloud computing is only now making a breakthrough in the business world. Companies predominantly benefit from cloud computing in that software, programming environments, or IT infrastructure can be accessed and used in the shortest possible time without having to wait for lengthy implementation and installation periods. At the same time, the offerings are usually low-maintenance (provided by a service provider), it can be scaled to virtually any size, it can be remunerated on a user-dependent basis, and it can be offered at a user-dependent price. However, certain challenges still need to be resolved in terms of costly integration into the IT landscape, limited customizing options, and SLAs that are often not tailored for the customer. Furthermore, a comparatively higher effort is required to secure data protection and data security, which is not a trivial task. As a side effect of the growing popularity of cloud computing, the so-called unofficial information systems (shadow IT) are emerging more and more in the business departments of certain companies. IT management guidelines need to be designed in such a way that it does not prevent agile and innovative behavior on the technical side and that they simultaneously take compliance and security requirements into account. Datev's security-as-a-service solution is an example of a business model innovation via cloud computing. The traditional business of Datev is to provide software to tax consultants, lawyers, as well as auditors and their clients. With its newly created cloud solution, Datev now also offers its clients centralized security infrastructure (including e-mail encryption, reverse proxy scanning) that protects the local IT environment from Internet attacks [6].

Mobile computing, which is a technological development that has been with us for some years, has had a particular impact on both the business world and private life in recent years. The use of mobile devices for telecommunication began more than 40 years ago when Motorola introduced the first mobile phone in 1973. The inventor of the mobile phone, Martin Cooper, made the first mobile phone call on 3 April 1973 when he called his rival at Bell Labs [7]. Since then, mobile telephone services developed consistently. According to the International Telecom Union (ITU), there were more than 7 billion mobile phone lines in 2015, which translates into roughly one mobile phone per inhabitant of our planet [8]. The development of a simple mobile phone into a smartphone, which experienced a major boost with the first Apple iPhone's market launch in 2007, is a major growth driver that can also be regarded as a milestone of the "digital revolution." Since then, these devices have become increasingly powerful (even more powerful than certain desktop PCs only a few years ago) and are now replacing numerous non-telecommunication related product categories, such as portable computers, organizers, PDAs, MP3 players, video games, navigation devices, torches, alarm clocks, and digital cameras. A major change on the consumer side—probably triggered by the smartphone's triumphant success—is the fact that such devices are becoming more and more seamlessly integrated into their users' everyday lives, due to, among other things, the simplest and most intuitive operation. Especially the development towards *always on* offers significant potential for new business models. The numerous other developments that aim to bind information processing closer to people, are also particularly interesting in this area. These include primarily wearables, such as intelligent watches, glasses, or even clothing, which—more and more—capture data from the user himself. Self-tracking automatically records and evaluates user movements, sleep phases, and body functions. The interaction between the various devices, applications, and data is becoming ever simpler and more convenient, due to new big data and cloud technologies.

The *Internet of things* is another technological driver of digitalization, which we have been discussing for a number of years. This trend shows that not only classic computers and mobile devices, but increasingly also machines and devices that do not belong to these categories, are connected to and communicate with the Internet.

Sensors and actuators are used to create cyber-physical systems out of analogous things—that is, a combination of mechanical parts, electronic parts, and information technology components—which thereby have a virtual representation in the networked world. Through their increased interconnectedness—also with humans, among other things—efforts are made to minimize the information gap between the real and virtual worlds. An increasing number of everyday devices, such as washing machines, sports equipment, vehicles, as well as locking and access systems, have embedded computers with networking capabilities. In similar vein, consumers can already buy curious, networked products, such as the HAPIfork, which is a smart fork with an integrated nutrition coach, or the Finnish company, Enevo's, smart recycling container, which regularly measures its filling level via ultrasonic measuring devices and sends the data to the Enevo server, which, in turn, organizes that the containers are emptied efficiently. The car manufacturer, Tesla, which regularly provides remote automatic software updates for its customers' automobiles, is currently also attracting a lot of attention.

In the corporate context, the Internet of things has attracted a lot of attention, especially under the term *Industry 4.0*. By this, we mean a production environment consisting of intelligent, self-controlling objects that are temporarily networked to perform specific tasks. In this specific context—analogous to the generic Internet of things—we are also referring to cyber-physical production systems with which we are moving ever closer to our vision of automated production [9]. By interconnecting production plants via the Internet, it becomes possible to integrate value creation chains in a completely new way. In the past, suppliers, manufacturing companies, and customers were mainly connected to each other via dispatching systems, but now it is possible to link production and logistics systems directly, which creates considerable potential for innovation. The companies Festo and Siemens, for example, are working on new intelligent multi-carrier systems that enable the implementation of fully-automated production processes at a batch size of one. Based on such concepts, the classic workshop and assembly line production merge, thereby enabling the manufacture of mass-produced products on a customer-specific basis [10].

The technological innovation that we would like to finally introduce here, are the intelligent systems. Intelligent systems result from a long-lasting maturation process, namely research work in the field of artificial intelligence (AI). The aim of the efforts was, and still is, to bestow a human-like intelligence on computers so that they can work independently on complex problems. In addition to the constantly improving algorithms, some of the innovations described above have also contributed to the upsurge of intelligent systems, such as the ability to process big data, as well as the establishment of cloud computing and the Internet of things. In contrast to what was originally planned and expected, the renaissance of the artificial intelligence idea is not based on individual systems, but predominantly on interconnected computer networks. Simple examples of intelligent systems that we have already integrated into our everyday lives, are semantic search engines, such as Wolfram Alpha or Google, which accept natural language as input and try to grasp the semantics of a question. Automatic speech assistants and dialog systems, such as Siri (Apple), Cortana (Microsoft), or Google Now (Alphabet), are also used more and more to control smartphones and other end devices. The development of self-driving cars demonstrates that the automotive industry is also affected by this development. Inspired by the pioneering work of certain universities and also Google with its driverless car, the majority of mass producers are now technologically able to produce vehicles that do not require manual control by a driver. Although a section of the A9 motorway in Bavaria already serves as a test track for the further development of autonomous driving, it will take a number of years to attend to the ethical issues and legal challenges before it is ready for mass production. In the corporate context, hopes are resting on the further development of robotics, that is, increasingly autonomous machines, and we are already experiencing it with Industry 4.0. IBM's Watson computer system, which attracted much attention in 2011 after beating two human opponents in the American quiz show Jeopardy, can be a solution for more extensive business-relevant applications. Since it can independently extract information from data and draw conclusions, Watson holds potential for future applications in areas such as customer service, health care, and the financial industry [11].

After introducing the central technological drivers of digitalization, the question arises: What are the core features of these innovations compared to previous technologies? As already stated above, the approaches that we presented are not necessarily revolutionary. Instead, their innovative strength stems from massively increased performance, significantly better networking possibilities, and the ever more widespread use. The increased performance is simply a result of increasingly cheaper and—therefore more usable—memory and ever faster processors. Devices are also becoming easier to interconnect and they can be expanded into faster computer networks. On the one hand, these developments lead to a new quantity and quality of data, the possibility of real-time processing, and multimedia data processing. On the other hand, the use of actuators and sensors enables an increasing autonomy of the used technology. In terms of distribution, the new technologies are characterized by a high ubiquity. In today's world, information technology reaches all spheres of its users' lives. These developments have resulted in almost limitless opportunities for the use of innovative information technologies, including and primarily for business purposes.

The Digital Revolution and Its Disruptive Effect

The current transformation of business and value creation models, which is driven by the above-mentioned and other technological innovations, is at present a "hot topic" under the keyword of digitalization. In the past, IT topics were rarely part of business discussions, but when you look at relevant business magazines nowadays, you almost get the impression of holding an IT magazine in your hand. By observing the companies, we quickly realized that digitalization plays a major role in strategy discussions and that it is often already addressed by ongoing projects. Many experts, especially those with an IT background, view this trend towards digitalization as exaggerated; at least the timing and intensity of the current discussions appear to be remarkable. An essential point of conflict is the digitalization concept. For example,

Wikipedia understands digitalization as "the process of converting information into a digital (i.e. computer-readable) format, in which the information is organized into bits." We, however, mean something different with the current trend towards digitalization.

Digitalization is the use of technological innovations in the business context with a significant influence on products, services, business processes, sales channels, and supply channels. The associated potential benefits include, among others, increased sales or productivity, innovations in value creation, and new forms of customer interaction. Thereby, digitalization has disruptive consequences for many companies and industries, to the extent that it is often not an option to continue an analogous business. Due to the far-reaching nature of these technological changes, we can expect these disruptive changes to be significantly more far-reaching than, for example, those that directly resulted in the introduction of the Internet. This can result in a formerly successful operating company losing its dominant position against its competitors in a short period of time. There are many examples of this in the past, such as Kodak and Nokia. Kodak, once the world's leading photography company, was too late in recognizing the transition from analogue to digital photography and quickly went bankrupt with its traditional business model [12]. A similar situation was also experienced by the mobile phone manufacturer Nokia, which was the world market leader in 2011, but is now only a niche player. Despite its strength in the traditional mobile phone market, Nokia was unable to keep up with its new competitors, Samsung and Apple, in the development of the smartphone [13]. In the age of digitalization, the companies therefore face the challenge to question the existing business models and to develop them further by using new technologies—or even to revolutionize them—in order to not fall victim to digitalization's disruptive power. The current danger that many companies currently feel exposed to can be summed up very nicely with a quotation from the American author Stewart Brand: "Once a new technology rolls over you, if you're not part of the steamroller, you're part of the road" [14].

How Business Can Benefit from the Digitalization Trend

Digitalization has enormous potential benefits for the business world. Many companies—especially young start-ups—expect business model innovations through the use of digital technologies. Examples of such business model innovations are the numerous business ideas of the sharing economy. Successful companies from this sector are mainly active in car sharing (e.g., car2go, DriveNow), mobility services (e.g., Uber), and shared housing (e.g., Airbnb, couchsurfing.org). The essential idea of this business concept is to share resources, which one does not need on a permanent basis, with other people. This approach is particularly attractive, because all parties involved benefit; the provider receives a gradual return on his investment, the consumer receives the service at a comparatively low price, and the operating platform typically receives a commission. From an economic point of view, shared consumption makes better use of scarce resources and, thus, reduces the quantity of goods without consumers having to lower their standard of living. The sharing economy also has ecological potential. A much-quoted example is the ordinary drill, which is, on average, used for 45 h during its lifetime in a private household, although more than 300 h would be possible without any problem [15].

Another opportunity for digitalization (which is simultaneously a threat to established market players) is the possibility for companies to enter established markets with new technological possibilities and to gain a foothold with their innovative offers. The automotive sector is an exemplary industry that is currently enormously influenced by new market participants. Tesla Motors, an American company that was founded only in 2003, has quickly become the market leader for luxury electric cars, while the established manufacturers in the field of electromobility are still lagging behind. Furthermore, it is actually not the established players who have driven the development of the already mentioned self-propelled car, but rather the technology companies such as Google and Apple. It will be interesting to see which vehicle brands will lead the market in the coming decades.

It appears that the financial industry is currently experiencing a similar development. In line with Bill Gates' hypothesis that "banking is necessary, banks are not," which was published as long ago as 1994, more and more start-ups are using modern products and services in an attempt to challenge large banks and financial service providers. Here, the young companies are particularly good at understanding their customers' needs in the digital world. In order to create their service range, they rely on the interaction of selected digital technologies such as social media, mobile computing, big data analytics, and cloud computing. The traditional players in the banking sector are afraid of losing business; they noticed these developments at a very late stage and are trying to counteract them with investments, some of which are even worth billions.

In addition to innovations at the business model level, digitalization is also expected to generate a high level of value creation for companies, especially in the production sector. Under the keyword *Industry 4.0* and following the guiding principle of *smart factory*, the next stage of industrial production automation by machines that communicate with each other and operate autonomously, is already underway. At the moment, it appears that this development is of great economic importance, which is why we are referring to the fourth industrial revolution—the next evolutionary stage after the introduction of mechanical production facilities that use water and steam power (first industrial revolution), the introduction of mass production based on electrical energy (second industrial revolution), and the use of electronics and information technology to further automate production (third industrial revolution). The factory of the future is self-organizing—thanks to communicating machines and components—and is networked with suppliers and customers. The smart factory therefore knows when a certain number of parts have to be produced—precursors and raw materials are ordered automatically. This results in huge flexibility that enables so-called "mass customization," namely the production of small batches or even customized products (batch size 1) at the price of comparable standard products [16]. The car manufacturer, Opel, is a good example of mass customization in the production sector. The customer who purchases an Opel Adam can individually choose the obligatory body color, the roof color, as well as the exterior mirrors, and the radiator grille. There are even numerous possibilities for individualizing the interior so that the vehicle can be adapted according to personal ideas in several hundred thousand ways [17].

The trend towards digitalization also opens up numerous new opportunities for marketing, sales, and customer service. First of all, the new technologies enable new channels for interacting with customers. Particularly the upsurge in social media resulted in a promising expansion of traditional marketing, sales, and service channels into new interaction media such as Facebook, Twitter, WhatsApp, or smartphone apps, especially for the young, but increasingly also for the older, target groups. As a result, customers' changing expectations regarding continuous availability can be met around the clock. Driven by the customers' experience in social networks and the smartphone users' "always on" mentality, companies are now expecting much shorter response times than a few years ago. As a result, companies are already relying more and more on online marketing and significantly stronger maintenance of their own websites, Facebook presences, and Twitter channels. The new campaign tool, "viral marketing," appears to be very promising in the digital world. Entertaining campaigns in the form of short videos or graphics are usually distributed in social networks and often include almost unobtrusive advertising messages. Successful campaigns then spread like a virus that is passed from user to user. A well-known example of a viral commercial is the video of the grocery chain Edeka, in which the Berlin artist Friedrich Liechtenstein sings the song "Supergeil" while dancing through supermarket aisles and living rooms [18]. After its release in February 2014, the video spread rapidly and by the end of 2015 it had been viewed more than 15 million times on Youtube. In addition to customers having more communication channels, the new digital technologies also help better understand the customer and his needs—especially through the use of big data analytics—and can thus address them in a more targeted manner. For example, the outdoor brand Columbia, used dynamic advertising banners on mobile websites that displayed the appropriate requests to buy—anything from flip-flops to rain jackets, depending on weather conditions—based on the user's location and the associated weather data [19]. A classic in this area is, of course, Amazon's buying recommendations, which are generated on the basis of earlier purchases, as well as the buying behavior of comparable customers, and then displayed on a customer-specific basis. These developments result in a much stronger focus on the customer than was the case a few years ago. The technological possibilities help companies and their marketing departments differentiate between potential and existing customers and provide them with information tailored to their specific needs. This also enables customer experience management that aims at turning satisfied customers into loyal customers and ultimately into ambassadors for a product or brand by creating positive customer experiences. As a result of the ever-increasing proximity to customers, companies in B2B retailing face the question whether it is not possible to sell the manufactured products directly to end customers without involving the retail trade as an intermediary. An attractive web shop or a well-designed app is often sufficient to reach a large number of potential customers.

German car manufacturers are, for example, already experimenting with network-based direct sales models, such as BMW's electric vehicles sales [20].

In our opinion, digitalization will also lead to a change in the organizational structure of certain companies—essentially to flatten the structure. The new communication channels via the use of social media are primarily responsible for this. They can be used to facilitate horizontal communication across departmental boundaries—even between employees who do not know each other personally. This means that normal, vertical communication via supervisors and reporting channels are becoming less important and that communication generally becomes less controllable. These developments can also lead to a new way of decision-making and management. Technologies such as big data, cloud computing, and the Internet of things can offer completely different information on which to base management decisions. All basic information is (almost) complete and always up-to-date ("real-time"). This enables the decision makers to develop a much larger number of action alternatives and to also evaluate them efficiently. These evaluations are no longer conducted by using simple decision models based on a large number of assumptions; they are conducted by means of hypothesis testing that is based on large empirical data sets. This, in turn, significantly increases the speed and quality of decision-making.

The potential benefits of digitalization at this stage relate to the design of the knowledge workplace, which is subject to changing requirements as a result of current developments in the economy, society, and information technology. The use of technological innovations opens up numerous new avenues for workplace design to meet these requirements. For example, modern, digital workplace concepts enable—depending on the specific working context—the distributed work to be carried out at any place and at any time; it also enables, more and more, self-determined workflows supported by a wide variety of device types. The digital workplace aims to increase employee productivity, enable new types of work, improve access to existing knowledge in the company, increase employee satisfaction, and improve employee innovation and creativity [21]. The pharmaceutical company, Merck, which has created a new digital workplace for its 39,000 employees worldwide, is an example of the "digital workplace of the future." Employees can now use an information, communication, and collaboration platform to communicate with each other, work together, and stay up to date in real time [22]. The reinsurance company, Munich Re, has also recently worked on the *next generation workplace*. The project initiative's goal is to enable employees to use their own devices or those provided by the company, as required, for working from any location—such as an office, the company campus, or even a home office. They aim to enable their employees to work together from any location in the world [23].

Digital Companies Are also Exposed to a Number of Risks

The transformation to a digital company does not only consist of positive aspects. A business that increasingly focuses on the innovative use of technologies is also exposed to numerous risks. Failure of the implemented technologies generally damages business and can, in extreme cases, put the existence of the company at risk. The concept of business continuity management will therefore become increasingly important in most companies. Digital companies are also particularly exposed to the dangers of cybercrime and industrial espionage, due to their high IT penetration. Well-developed security management therefore becomes a central skill for preventing such possible incidents. Since many digital business models are based on the processing of private data, data security and data protection both become critical business tasks. When personal data is not handled in a sensitive manner, the digital company will most likely lose customers (although we currently observe the opposite phenomenon on Google and Facebook). The increased transparency of business models associated with digitalization also increases the risk of business model imitations and new competitors. A clear brand message and building a solid reputation can counteract such risks. Last but not least, recruiting and retaining suitable employees become an ongoing challenge. Developing and operating digital businesses require very specific employee skills and only a few people currently have it.

Implications of Digitalization for IT Management

Although digitalization is a phenomenon that is strongly driven by information technology, it appears from the above statements that business functions are in the foreground. Nevertheless, it remains an IT topic. This raises the question of how the future IT department will be able to cope with these changed contextual conditions and how it will facilitate, support, or even drive the stronger IT use that digitalization requires. From the IT department's point of view, digitalization poses several challenges at different levels. First of all, it must remain up to date with technological changes. Understanding the new technologies, assessing their potential applications, and, if necessary, mastering them, is crucially important. The IT department must simultaneously develop its own role in the company. At present, many IT departments view themselves as pure service providers and are often also perceived as such. Although IT innovations are implemented, it usually occurs reactively in response to the business units' requirements, or incrementally as technological improvements to existing technological solutions. However, for digitalization, they must assume a new role with a further reach and pitch it as such in the organization. This involves anchoring and representing the IT department's function at company management level. In order to develop IT-based innovations for digitalization, this also includes the development of skills, structures, and processes. Furthermore, the issue of suitable architectures also arises. IT innovations are easier to implement—especially if they require integration into an existing IT landscape—if the existing architecture is flexible, modular, and elastic. Here, appropriate preparations are also necessary. After all, IT departments—as is the case with the entire digital company—also need the necessary employees to implement digital change. Digitalization requires additional and different resources than those that are conventionally available to the current IT departments. Employees who develop new products, services, and business models need different skills and talents, and often also a different education compared to those in the "analog" business. In the following chapter, we will place the changed requirements for the IT department and its management in historical context. We will then show and briefly explain our theses about the IT department of the future.

Overview: The Digital Revolution
- At present, the business models and value creation chains of the business world are changing drastically.
- New technologies such as big data analytics, social media, cloud computing, mobile computing, the Internet of things, and intelligent machines trigger current developments.
- Digitalization means the use of technological innovations in the business context that significantly influences products, services, business processes, sales channels, and supply channels.
- Digitalization has disruptive consequences for many companies and industries; continuing as an analog business is often not an option.
- Companies benefit from digitalization in terms of new business models and markets, value-added innovations, new opportunities for marketing and sales, new communication channels, new types of decision-making, and new ways of shaping the knowledge workplace.
- The digital enterprise is also exposed to a number of risks, particularly in terms of technology availability, security, and data protection.
- Digitalization has a significant impact on IT departments and their management.

References

1. McRae, H. (2015, March 5). Facebook, Airbnb, Uber, and the unstoppable rise of the content non-generators. *Independent*. http://www.independent.co.uk/news/business/comment/hamish-mcrae/facebook-airbnb-uber-and-the-unstoppable-rise-of-the-content-non-generators-10227207.html
2. Mattern, F., Huhn, W., Perrey, J., Dörner, K., Lorenz, J.-T., & Spillecke, D. (2012, May). *Turning buzz into gold – How pioneers create value from social media*. New York: McKinsey & Company.
3. McKendrick, J. (2015, March 17). Digital technologies will soon add $1 trillion-plus to global economy. *Forbes/Tech*. http://www.forbes.com/sites/joemckendrick/2015/03/17/digital-technologies-will-soon-add-1-trillion-plus-to-global-economy/
4. BlueYonder. (2018, April 18). *Kaiser's Tengelmann automates replenishment*. https://www.blue-yonder.com/en/customers/kaiserstengelmann-demand-forecast-and-replenishment

5. Harris, J., Ives, B., & Junglas, I. (2012). IT consumerization: When gadgets turn into enterprise IT tools. *MIS Quarterly Executive, 11*(23), 99–112.
6. BITKOM. (2013). *Wie Cloud Computing neue Geschäftsmodelle ermöglicht. Leitfaden.* https://www.bitkom.org/Publikationen/2014/Leitfaden/Wie-Cloud-Computing-neue-Geschaeftsmodelle-ermoeglicht/140203-Wie-Cloud-Computing-neue-Geschaeftsmodelle-ermoeglicht.pdf
7. Green, B. (2011, April 3). 38 years ago he made the first cell phone call. *CNN.* http://edition.cnn.com/2011/OPINION/04/01/greene.first.cellphone.call/
8. ITU. (2015, May). *The world in 2015 ICT facts and figures.* https://www.itu.int/en/ITU-D/Statistics/Documents/facts/ICTFactsFigures2015.pdf
9. BITKOM. (2014). *Industrie 4.0 – Volkswirtschaftliches Potenzial für Deutschland. Studie.* https://www.bitkom.org/Publikationen/2014/Studien/Studie-Industrie-4-0-Volkswirtschaftliches-Potenzial-fuer-Deutschland/Studie-Industrie-40.pdf
10. VDMA. (2015, April). *Industrie 4.0 konkret – Lösungen für die industrielle Praxis.* http://hm.vdma.org/documents/10181/20674/I40_Broschuere.pdf/5d4ae916-1e7b-4320-a769-10e985abb3b9
11. IBM. (2015). *From deep blue to Watson.* http://www-05.ibm.com/de/watson/
12. Spiegel Online. (2012, January 19). *Fotokonzern am Ende: Wie Kodak aus unserem Leben verschwand.* http://www.spiegel.de/netzwelt/gadgets/fotokonzern-am-ende-wie-kodak-aus-unserem-leben-verschwand-a-810043.html
13. Focus Online. (2012, June 14). *Hintergrund: Aufstieg und Niedergang von Nokia.* http://www.focus.de/digital/computer/telekommunikation-hintergrund-aufstieg-und-niedergang-von-nokia_aid_767328.html
14. Brand, S. (1987). *The media lab: Inventing the future at MIT.* New York: Viking.
15. Leismann, K., Schmitt, M., Rohn, H., & Baedeker, C. (2012). *Nutzen statt Besitzen – Auf dem Weg zu einer ressourcenschonenden Konsumkultur* (Vol. 27, *Schriften zur Ökologie*). Heinrich-Böll-Stiftung. https://www.boell.de/de/content/nutzen-statt-besitzen-auf-dem-weg-zu-einer-ressourcenschonenden-konsumkultur
16. Denner, V. (2014, December 12). Industrie 4.0 – Der Schlüssel zum Erfolg. *Handelsblatt.* http://www.handelsblatt.com/technik/das-technologie-update/energie/industrie-4-0-der-schluessel-zum-erfolg/11114444.html
17. Opel. (2014, September). Creating unique vehicles. *Opel Post.* https://opelpost.com/09/2014/creating-unique-vehicles/
18. Löhr, J. (2014, März 25). Virales marketing: Werbung wie ein Grippevirus. *FAZ.* http://www.faz.net/aktuell/wirtschaft/unternehmen/virales-marketing-werbung-wie-ein-grippevirus-12863548.html
19. Puscher, F. (2015, September 21). Kreativer Einsatz von Daten im Online Marketing: 10 Beispiele für BigData-Kampagnen, die verblüffen. *E8 Magazin.* https://www.e8magazin.de/kreativer-einsatz-von-daten-im-online-marketing-10-beispiele-fuer-bigdata-kampagnen-die-verblueffen/
20. Roland Berger Strategy Consultants. (2015, March 17). *Die Digitale Transformation der Industrie.* http://www.rolandberger.de/media/pdf/Roland_Berger_Analysen_zur_Studie_Digitale_Transformation_20150317.pdf
21. Urbach, N., & Ahlemann, F. (2016). Der Wissensarbeitsplatz der Zukunft: Trends, Herausforderungen und Implikationen für das strategische IT-Management. *HMD – Praxis der Wirtschaftsinformatik, 53*(1), 16–28.
22. Kurzlechner, W. (2015, November 26). Collaboration: Merck baut digitalen Arbeitsplatz der Zukunft. *CIO.* http://www.cio.de/a/merck-baut-digitalen-arbeitsplatz-der-zukunft,3250198
23. Freimark, A. (2014, June 11). Arbeitsplatz 2020: Munich Re baut den Next Generation Workplace. *CIO.* http://www.cio.de/a/munich-re-baut-den-next-generation-workplace,2958161

The Development of Corporate IT: From the Beginnings to the IT Department of the Future

Due to the trend towards digitalization that is described in the previous chapter, it is crucial for many companies to successfully, effectively, and efficiently produce innovative business and value creation models, to develop appropriate IT solutions, and to realign their own companies in order to remain competitive. In this context, the concerned IT departments are called upon to play a proactive role in the innovation process and to accompany, or even drive, the changes regarding the necessary IT support. At present, however, the majority of IT departments do not yet fulfill this role completely, because they—as reactive service providers—often do not have the structures, processes, or skills to systematically develop (business) innovations. Furthermore, IT departments are often perceived as bureaucratic, inflexible, and not on an equal footing with the business departments. For example, in the event that business departments request short-term changes to information systems, the changes are not implemented quickly enough—from their point of view—if the IT department's timeframe for making the changes is too long. However, in the digitalization context, the ability to quickly modify information systems is of great importance. The question that arises at this point is why it appears as if corporate IT, in many cases, is not optimally positioned for the challenges of the digital transformation. In order to answer this question, we need to give an overview of the most important development steps in corporate IT. Understanding this history, should help better determine the changes that are necessary for the digital transformation.

Corporate IT from the 1950s to the Present Day

Corporate IT has undergone a number of developments since its beginning. Its main focus was primarily on the operation of mainframes, followed by the management of increasingly networked personal computing, and finally industrialized IT management.

The mainframe era can be considered as the first era of corporate IT. The early IBM chairman, Thomas Watson, of all people, is credited with the popular misguided prediction in 1943 that *"there is a world market for maybe five computers"* [1]. The reason for this opinion was that the first generations of computers were still tube computers with enormous power consumption and a latent susceptibility to failure. During the mid-1950s, with the invention of the transistor, the first mainframe computers entered the organizational environment—initially predominantly in research facilities and in the military context, and then also in companies. These computers were not physically comparable to the modern mainframe systems of today. The first generations occupied entire rooms, which had to be air-conditioned to counteract the heat generated by the appliances. Operating these machines was relatively complicated and costly. In addition to software developers who, as is the case at present, designed the programs, the operators were exclusively responsible for operating the computer system. The first mainframe computers could only be fed input data via punched cards, which required a specific reader to read and eventually store the data on a magnetic tape. Then, the actual mainframe computer processed the magnetic tape and stored the output on another magnetic tape. In the final stage, a printer transferred the calculated results from the magnetic tape to paper [2]. Back then, the main focus was on using the computers' computing capacity, which was extremely high at the time; they could simply calculate faster than humans. However, compared to today's computers, the area of application was very limited. The mainframes essentially performed their computing tasks only for very well-structured problems that had comparatively simple algorithms. The computers could, however, be used at a relatively early stage for material requirements planning (MRP) and later for enterprise resource planning (ERP). In the past, IT management predominantly focused on operating and maintaining the mainframes. However, project management tasks in application development increasingly became part of IT management. In the mid-1960s, the phenomenon of the software crisis emerged—for the first time, software costs exceeded hardware costs. As a consequence, the first major failed software projects occurred, which resulted in the establishment of software engineering [3]. Despite high expenditure, there was generally little pressure for justifying corporate IT, because the competitive advantages of companies with a high level of IT penetration were largely undisputed.

The second era of corporate IT began when the first personal computers (PC) emerged in the 1970s. The main drivers of these changes were the market launches of the microprocessor and semiconductor memory. As a result, the size of computers could be reduced to such an extent that they could be set up quite easily at or near an office workstation and, thus, be assigned to employees "personally" [4]. From the perspective of the mainframe era, this development was like a revolution, although the idea that a computer could also find its place in private households, was initially dismissed as absurd. Even in 1977, Ken Olson, founder of the renowned computer company, DEC, drew attention with the remarkable quote *"there is no reason why anyone would want a computer in their home"* [1]. Eventually, however, the PC spread quite quickly—in both the professional and private contexts—with Apple I (market entry in 1976), Apple II (1977), Commodore PET (1977), and the IBM PC (1981). Compared to the mainframe, one of the PC's crucial advancements was that the (trained) layman could use a "desk computer" without too much difficulty. As a result, the use of word processing and spreadsheet programs, among others, meant that particularly office tasks were automated. Furthermore, group communication became considerably easier, due to increased networking, as well as the introduction of e-mail and various collaboration tools. These new solutions, however, soon reached their limits. At that stage, the processing power of the PCs was such that it is not remotely comparable to that of today's computer generations (and not even with that of modern smartphones). The computers were increasingly interconnected, but mostly only in local networks. The technology of that time can generally, from today's perspective, be regarded as rather immature, especially in terms of performance and stability. The availability of application systems was also very limited, especially at the beginning of the PC age. Overall, it appears that the management of the technology was difficult during that time. For IT management, the new era meant not only the operation of data processing centers, but also the management of workstations, which was particularly challenging, considering the stability and reliability of the systems that were used. Application development, which has also become increasingly complex and time-consuming, required increasingly professional project management. Since computers were relocated to the workplace, IT management has increasingly taken on information management tasks. Even during this phase, the IT department's importance within companies was largely undisputed, because well-functioning IT equipment at the workplace contributed to the employees' increased productivity and also to the attractiveness of the workplace—although the IT staff's customer orientation could be improved in many cases.

During the mid-1990s, the third era of corporate IT finally began—the age of IT industrialization. This phase can be viewed as a result of companies being increasingly penetrated with information technology. Over the years, hardware, software, and cross-company networking have become more cost-effective. As the focus increasingly shifted to client-server architectures and the corresponding applications, the classic mainframes lost more and more of their importance. The simple workstation computer developed further into a multimedia PC and became the central communication medium for office workers—at the latest, with the widespread establishment of the Internet. The first Internet-based business models were established under the banner of e-commerce, which increasingly began to threaten standard, bricks-and-mortar commerce. These developments led to a rapid increase in the number of application systems used by companies, as well as increasingly complex company architectures. Information technology has developed into an essential business resource. The IT budgets also grew concurrently—but with the IT departments' service orientation still remaining at a low level. This resulted in more and more debates about whether IT is still a resource that sets the company apart from the competition or whether it has already become a "commodity," which—similar to electrical energy—is business-critical, but does not have any competitive advantages. These debates got off to a flying start with the widely acclaimed article "IT doesn't matter" by the US-American author and business journalist, Nicholas G. Carr, which was published during May 2003 in the Harvard Business Review [5] and shortly afterwards as a book [6]. Carr argued that, with ever decreasing costs and ever better availability, the use of information technology is no longer a strategic advantage. He accordingly recommended that corporate management should spend less money on IT infrastructure and not always use the latest solutions. As one can easily imagine, Carr's propositions caused a huge controversy. There were, of course, also numerous examples of companies that had already gained enormous competitive advantages through the use of information technology and, thus, immediately suppressed the established market participants one after the other—here, we can refer to Amazon or, later, Apple with iTunes. Nevertheless, corporate IT was increasingly forced to justify itself during this period, which eventually led to transforming industrial methods and processes to information technology. The main goal of this IT industrialization was to increase the effectiveness and efficiency of the IT departments and to position them as service-oriented service providers. It quickly became clear that the often-prevailing plan-build-run paradigm could no longer adequately reflect the reality of IT departments. Instead of planning systems extensively and then using an in-house IT department to implement them, more and more companies started to shorten their IT value creation chain by handing over parts of this chain to external partners. Accordingly, many IT departments continued to evolve in the direction of a source-make-deliver paradigm [7] (see chapter "Development and operation are not decisive: IT management follows the "innovate-design-transform" paradigm"). This development means that it became necessary for IT management to develop new skills. The classic IT tasks, such as IT infrastructure operation and application development, were increasingly pushed into the background. Since then, distinctive competencies in areas such as IT service management, the prioritization of IT investments within the context of portfolio management, the management of IT architectures, requirements management, as well as connecting customers, suppliers, and partners have become more popular. In many cases, IT industrialization had the desired effects—but at the same time it also resulted in certain companies' IT departments presently operating far removed from the business, thereby making an intact business-IT alignment a continuous challenge. Now that the digitalization trend has shown that Carr's propositions are probably not correct and that IT—when used correctly—actually has huge potential for business (see chapter "The digital revolution: how technological trends change the business world"), it appears that corporate IT is no longer optimally set up for the new challenges.

Current Challenges of Digitalization

With digitalization and the resulting noticeable increase in the importance of information technology for companies, the demands on corporate IT have changed. Information technology is no longer understood "only" as a business-critical resource, because a large part of the business processes depend on it; it is increasingly also understood as a central component of new products, services, and even complete business models. As a result, the use of IT not only makes business operations more efficient; business operations are no longer conceivable without IT. Although many IT organizations have thus far concentrated on transforming their departments' requirements as effectively and efficiently as possible into high-quality IT services and then operating them accordingly, they are now increasingly challenged to actively shape the entire company. Since information technologies are nowadays increasingly used to implement business innovations,—which will specifically continue in future—IT departments need to cooperate proactively and at an early stage with the various business units to jointly design and launch such innovations. Concepts such as co-location, IT innovation management, and functional architecture management can be understood as early signs of a "new IT" that discards the role of a mere IT service provider and adopts the role of consultant, enabler, and innovator. However, developments such as cloud computing or industry-specific process standardization make it easier to outsource elements of the IT value chain. IT infrastructure management, the development of new software, as well as IT operations can, thus, be entrusted to comparatively uncomplicated, specialized providers who have the necessary skills and can realize economies of scale. These developments bring about a gradual shift in the roles and capabilities of today's IT departments and it appears that this will be reflected in the structures, processes, methods, and governance mechanisms. Corporate IT and its management must realign themselves to meet digitalization requirements. The generally assumed paradox here is that the IT department would largely eliminate itself in the current set-up if it took the implications of digitalization seriously. However, we believe that corporate IT is well advised to address the necessary developments in timely and proactive ways. If they do not play an active role in shaping the change process, they will not play a decisive role in digitalization and then they will eventually be replaced by external service providers.

Ten Hypotheses About the IT Department of the Future

In order to meet the current challenges of digitalization, it is necessary to significantly change the organizational, procedural, human resources, and cultural aspects. Certain companies are already responding to current changes, as well as those expected in future. However, it is often still unclear in which direction corporate IT should develop. In this book, we describe our view of the future IT department and give pointers for sustainable positioning. To this end, we formulated ten hypotheses to show in which areas significant changes can be expected. In the following section we give an overview of these hypotheses and in the subsequent chapters we discuss each one individually and in detail.

Hypothesis 1 No business without IT: IT is the central and indispensable driver of entrepreneurial value creation

At present, information technology is already an important production factor in most companies. However, it is often not considered as a strategically important competitive factor. We presume that this will change significantly as a result of the digital transformation. IT know-how will be required throughout the entire company. The use of IT no longer applies only to business processes, but increasingly also to the products and services that are offered. IT is therefore becoming a vital resource; the (usually theoretical) period from system failure to corporate insolvency will be drastically shortened. IT will be significantly more comprehensive, interconnected, autonomous and, above all, more creative. For the successful companies of the future, the existing business models are often only a starting point for further business development. They will accordingly need IT solutions even faster in future. The faster these IT solutions are specified, implemented, and put into operation, the better the companies will succeed in conquering markets and securing competitive positions. As a result of this development, today's business-IT alignment will evolve into a fusion of business and IT.

Hypothesis 2 Development and operation are not decisive: IT management follows the "innovate-design-transform" paradigm

Classic corporate IT is usually characterized by the relatively static *plan-build-run* paradigm, which structures the workflows and processes within IT departments and aligns them to increase efficiency. Fixed IT structures enable efficient workflows and promote automation, but they are limited when it comes to driving innovation. However, precisely this innovation activity, which leads to new or changed IT-based business and value creation models, is an essential task of digital transformation. We therefore propose the new *innovate-design-transform* paradigm with which IT departments can become the innovation drivers in their companies. At the core of this is a focus on innovation capability through greater agility and flexibility, the customer-oriented design capability of IT solutions for specific purposes, as well as the transformation capability to drive and implement the changes that result from digitalization. Due to the proposed paradigm shift, classic IT tasks such as the development and operation of application systems are fading even further into the background and are supplemented by new functions.

Hypothesis 3 Shadow IT as a lived practice: IT innovations are developed in interdisciplinary teams within the business departments

Nowadays, the business units initiate many IT projects, which are reactively implemented by the IT department. Due to relatively slow coordination and implementation processes, as well as long development cycles, the resulting IT solutions are often not innovative and rarely disruptive. Corporate IT is perceived as a slow service provider rather than a creative innovator. As a result of the digital transformation's increased pressure for change and the ever more convenient sourcing possibilities offered by cloud computing, the business units are becoming increasingly active—independently and without involving corporate IT—in terms of IT solutions. As a result of this detachment, the phenomenon of "individual data processing" or "shadow IT" arises, which is viewed as problematic for compliance, security, and architectural requirements. In this context, we ask ourselves whether this organizational separation of IT and business is appropriate in the light of digitalization. We come to the conclusion that IT innovations should ideally be created where they will be used later on—in the business departments. To this end, experts from all relevant areas should be involved and should work together. This makes the "official shadow IT" a lived practice.

Hypothesis 4 Innovations through networks: turning strategic suppliers into innovation partners

For more than 25 years, companies have focused on traditional IT outsourcing with a view to reduce costs or improve quality. In recent years, cloud sourcing has also established itself as a relatively new type of sourcing option, which comes very close to the vision of "IT from the wall socket." The central idea of sourcing IT services externally has traditionally been to outsource non-strategic parts of corporate IT in order to focus more specifically on activities that differentiate the company from its competitors. We presume that the trend towards outsourcing commodity IT will continue to intensify (see Hypothesis 6). At the same time, we presume that selected strategic suppliers will become innovation partners to further advance the companies as a central driving force. In the medium term, very few companies from traditional (non-IT) industries will have the necessary technological know-how to launch their IT innovations. This know-how will, however, be crucial for independently reaching sustainable success in the digital world. Accordingly, eye-to-eye technology partners will be required to develop innovations together with the commissioning companies. The partners that fill the competence gaps will increasingly participate in the business success of the developed innovations.

Hypothesis 5 Focusing on the user: development processes are agile, end-user centered, and merged with the operation

In many companies, software development processes are usually organized according to the waterfall model. This means that the different development phases are sequentially carried out, starting with the requirements assessment and then followed by the functional and technical conception, the implementation, the test, and the go-live—usually with minimal feedback possibilities between the phases. The development activities focus strongly on technology, products, and functions; user needs and acceptance have, thus far, received little attention. This procedure suits the requirements of the digital world only to a limited extent. If the traditional software development processes from the corporate context were applied to the development of a modern app in the consumer context, this would produce an update only every few months or even years. The app would, accordingly, not succeed in the market, because users are now accustomed to continuous background updates—and therefore to continuous up-to-date applications. We foresee a significantly greater spread of agile approaches in future, especially for the development of the "lightweight IT," which are front-end dominated, and end-customer oriented systems. A central idea of the agile approach is that the first deployment of rudimentary solutions occurs at a very early stage and these are then further developed iteratively by taking user feedback into consideration. Generally, the user will figure much more significantly in the foreground of development activities. Last but not least, software development and operation will continue to merge.

Hypothesis 6 Infrastructure as commodity: IT infrastructure services are traded on free markets and purchased as required

Despite the concept of outsourcing IT, which has been established for several years now, the classic IT operation at a significant number of companies still turns, to a large extent, on their own hardware in the internal data processing center—often with the support of third parties. Companies that already use cloud computing have, thus far, generally only relied on the internal "private cloud." The reluctance to purchase IT services externally is based on (historical) assumptions concerning the performance of wide area networks, the need for company-specific solutions, as well as the requirements for data protection, data security, and stability, which, in our opinion, no longer apply or only apply to a limited extent. We therefore expect an almost complete outsourcing of IT infrastructure services in future. These services can be procured via exchange-type markets in which, depending on supply and demand, prices for standardized infrastructure services are updated on a daily basis. For this purpose, these infrastructure services need to be standardized both technically and functionally. They also need to be decoupled from specific applications. In this way, IT infrastructure services can be purchased and consumed—easily and dynamically—in future.

Hypothesis 7 Digitalization as a risk: security and business continuity management are central cross-divisional functions of the company

With the growing penetration of information technology, companies in the digital world depend increasingly on the availability of their IT systems. However, the easy accessibility of systems via the Internet also leads to a particular vulnerability. Depending on the sector and business model (e.g., banks or stock exchanges), a completely failed system can already be the end of the affected company. Furthermore, IT will influence the physical well-being of individuals more and more as they move into digital products and services—for example, the self-driving automobile, robots in the care sector, or autonomous control systems in power plants. We observe, however, that many companies still underestimate IT risks and that these risks are therefore often not completely under control. One of the main reasons for this is undoubtedly the fact that IT security problems still have limited scope. However, as security problems are becoming more critical, we observe that effective IT security and business continuity management, which can be organized as cross-divisional functions in a company, are central competencies for sustainable business activity. Security competence development thus becomes an essential task of digital business.

Hypothesis 8 Transformable IT landscapes: IT architectures are standardized, modular, flexible, ubiquitous, elastic, cost-effective, and secure

For the past several years, the historically evolved IT infrastructure and application landscapes have been a major challenge for IT management. The "uncontrolled growth" prevalent in many companies often leads to a loss of transparency, increased risks and costs, distraction from problems in the core business, as well as an inability to flexibly implement new business strategies. Standardization efforts, advanced architecture concepts (such as service-oriented architectures and virtualization), and enterprise architecture management (EAM) can help some organizations address these challenges. Often, however, the problems are not actually solved and therefore the IT architectures of many companies are unsuitable, from our point of view, for agile digitalization projects. The new requirements of digital transformation demand IT landscapes that are much easier to transform. The standardization of IT architectures will therefore continue and—with the exception of competitively differentiated areas—will also extend to applications and business processes. Modularization approaches and flexible interface technologies will also become even more widespread. Particularly IT infrastructures will gain elasticity through the use of cloud technologies. Cost efficiency and security are necessary preconditions for the competitive use of IT.

Hypothesis 9 The end of the IT department: IT experts become part of the business departments and are coordinated by a dedicated executive responsibility

Influenced by the era of IT industrialization, corporate IT is usually positioned as an effective and efficient service provider, but is often perceived as "remote" from business and not very innovative. It is seldom seen as a business partner on an equal footing. Following the *plan-build-run* paradigm, the range of the IT departments' tasks is divided into three main phases. This includes identifying customer requirements and planning IT service availability, project initiation and implementation, as well providing services. We have already pointed out—with our previous hypotheses—that demand- and innovation-oriented activities in interdisciplinary teams gain more when they take place directly in the business units (see Hypothesis 3). The reason for this is that development and operation activities are less crucial, because specialized providers can perform them better for various reasons (see Hypothesis 4) and because IT infrastructure will, in future, be largely sourced from the clouds (see Hypothesis 6). The central question at this stage is whether a classic IT department makes sense at all. The answer, from our point of view, is: No. Corporate IT's remaining activities are predominantly long-term planning of IT architecture (architecture management), control and monitoring (innovation, project portfolio, and supplier management as well as service monitoring), as well as coordination tasks concerning decentralized and centralized IT-related tasks (IT governance, standardization). It is our considered opinion that these responsibilities are better suited for a central management function, which—in view of information technology becoming increasingly important for business—should be anchored close to the executive board.

Hypothesis 10 Demography, digital natives, and individual entrepreneurship: employees become a strategic competitive factor

Access to well-trained human resources is viewed as a key factor for the success of current and future digitalization initiatives. Specific qualifications and skills are needed to meet the new challenges that companies expect to face in the digital transformation. However, due to current demographic developments and changing personal requirements, especially of younger employees, companies find it increasingly difficult to identify and retain suitable employees. This challenge is particularly great for the IT-related tasks of digitalization, because not nearly enough young people receive training in technical professions. Furthermore, compared to previous generations of employees, the desire for individuality and self-determination influences the value system of new employees much stronger. These developments have a massive impact on the recruitment and retention of good IT staff, and dedicated HR management should respond by developing an attractive corporate culture and future-oriented business.

In the following chapters, we will present these hypotheses in more detail and we will discuss them comprehensively. We will particularly explain how these changes come about and why, from our point of view, they are unavoidable.

Overview: The Development of Corporate IT

- Digital transformation requires IT departments that play a proactive role in the innovation process and that accompany or even drive the necessary changes.
- At present, however, most IT departments do not yet fulfill this role, since they, as reactive service providers, have neither the structures, nor the necessary processes or capabilities.
- The historical view of corporate IT explains how this came about.
- Initially, corporate IT mainly focused on the operation of mainframes, followed by the management of increasingly interconnected personal computing, and finally industrialized IT management.
- In order to play a decisive role in the digital transformation, their own function needs to develop further in a timely and pro-active way.
- This requires organizational, procedural, personnel, and cultural changes, which we describe in our ten hypotheses for the future IT department.

References

1. Manhart, K. (2015, December 22). Die schlimmsten IT-Fehler: Die zehn größten IT-Irrtümer und -Fehlprognosen. *Tecchannel.de.* http://www.tecchannel.de/server/hardware/466465/it_irrtuemer_fehlprognosen_fehlentscheidungen_manager_fehler_computer/
2. Wikipedia. (2018). *Mainframe computer.* https://en.wikipedia.org/wiki/Mainframe_computer
3. Naur, P., & Randell, B. (1968, October 7–11). *Software engineering.* Report of a conference sponsored by the NATO Science Committee, Garmisch. http://homepages.cs.ncl.ac.uk/brian.randell/NATO/nato1968.pdf
4. Wikipedia. (2018, April 18). *Personal computer.* https://en.wikipedia.org/wiki/Personal_Computer
5. Carr, N. (2003, May). IT doesn't matter. *Harvard Business Review,* 5–12.
6. Carr, N. (2004). *Does IT matter? Information technology and the corrosion of competitive advantage.* Boston: Harvard Business School Press.
7. Zarnekow, R., Brenner, W., & Pilgram, U. (2006). *Integrated information management—Applying successful industrial concepts in IT.* Heidelberg: Springer.

No Business Without IT: IT Is the Central and Indispensable Driver of Entrepreneurial Value Creation

Information technology is already an important production factor in the majority of companies. In certain industries, IT has also become a strategic resource without which business activity is unthinkable. Banks and insurance companies are examples of this. So, what is new? In order to understand how important IT is for the future, it is necessary to understand how today's information technology can radically transform value creation and support processes in companies. We presume that, as a result of the digital transformation, IT know-how will be necessary throughout the company. The use of IT will no longer only apply to business processes, but increasingly also to the products and services on offer. IT is therefore becoming a resource that is essential for survival. IT will become significantly more comprehensive, interconnected, autonomous and, above all, creative. Successful future companies often use existing business models only as a starting point for further business development. Accordingly, the demand for faster IT solutions will be even higher in future. The faster they are specified, implemented, and put into operation, the better the companies will succeed in conquering markets and securing competitive positions.

The Influence of Information Technology Up to the Present

At present, information technology is mainly used to support business processes and to solve well-structured or semi-structured decision-making problems. This makes established business processes more efficient and effective. Efficiency is increased, for example, by automating or eliminating process steps, quickly transmitting information, or reducing media disruptions. Increased effectiveness can be achieved through advanced, computer-based decision models, automated reporting, or sophisticated data analysis. The basis for this progress was laid by powerful client-server systems—often still in use—, which were mostly developed into web applications.

N. Urbach, F. Ahlemann, *IT Management in the Digital Age*, Management for Professionals, https://doi.org/10.1007/978-3-319-96187-3_3

These are complemented by the benefits resulting from the connectivity of customers, suppliers, and business partners. Cost-effective wide area networks—in most cases the Internet—serve as the foundation. With protocols and languages such as TCP/IP, HTTP, or XML it is easier than ever before to integrate systems across organizational boundaries and to tightly interlink companies along supply chains. This trend is further enhanced by the increasing use of mobile devices. The changes that result from these developments already have very far-reaching consequences. Thereby, it is already possible to bypass intermediaries so that entire business models can become obsolete. This is patently obvious in retail and wholesale businesses, which came to a complete standstill in many sectors or whose business volumes decreased continuously over long periods of time. The over-the-counter book trade or media businesses, such as those for CDs and DVDs, are well-known examples. Almost everyone is familiar with the disruptive and transformational effects of digital companies such as Amazon, eBay, Apple, and Google, which have created new business models or made traditional business models obsolete [1]. However, the forthcoming changes that will result from the digital transformation will be much more far-reaching in many industries and business sectors.

Current Technology Trends and Their Influence on Business

Chapter "The digital revolution: how technological trends change the business world" of this book outlines that a number of very powerful technologies and technological concepts are currently maturing and that they are increasingly used in a business context. They include big data, cloud computing, social media, and the Internet of things. These technologies have the potential to penetrate companies' economic activities in a way that is hard to conceive in today's world. The disruptive effects are not actually unfolded by the concepts themselves, but rather by the basic characteristics of the technological parameters. It is necessary to bear in mind that new, groundbreaking technological innovations will continue to drive digitalization in the next few years. However, current and future technological developments have fundamental characteristics in common, namely the virtual infinity of information processing and, increasingly, also knowledge processing.

First, we observe a *never-ending generation of information*. Almost limitless possibilities of capturing the real world digitally (or virtually) ("Internet of things") arise from the fact that, in future, practically all areas of life will be digitally infiltrated and computer-aided devices will be increasingly equipped with sensors. Cameras, motion sensors, sensors for the measurement of vital functions, tracking devices, temperature sensors, as well as the various sensors installed in production facilities, are only a few examples of the technological possibilities that are already available. In certain device categories, the number of sensors has grown exponentially for some time now, for example in turbines and power plants, cars, or oil platforms. For example, the Airbus A380's engine automatically sends status information to Rolls Royce—worldwide and independent of the aircraft's other on-board electronics [2]. In addition, many devices are interconnected, thereby facilitating information retrieval. Even clothing and everyday objects are increasingly equipped with sensors, for example to support sporting activities or to increase entertainment value. In view of present developments, this trend will probably not slow down in the foreseeable future. On the contrary, in the years ahead we expect an even stronger growth in the use of sensors of all kinds.

Second, it is already possible to certify *unlimited storage of information* for many application domains. Falling prices of storage capacity and comprehensive cloud computing options on offer are harbingers of a time when data storage will be virtually unlimited [3]. For the majority of applications, the available storage will either be sufficient, or will not be a limitation. This development is facilitated by the fact that many relevant data stocks can be obtained or referenced externally without the need for in-house storage. Therefore, the company itself does not store consumer, geological, or even competitive data, but simply retrieves it from specialized service providers when it is needed. This means that an enormous amount of virtual data is available without needing a single hard disk drive within the company on which to store it. The same applies to open social media platforms (e.g., Facebook), advertising services (e.g., Google Ads), online encyclopedia/knowledge resources (e.g., Wikipedia), or general search queries (e.g., Google search). Furthermore, thanks to cloud computing, it will be possible—more than ever before—to externally request storage capacity at very competitive prices.

The phenomenon of *information that can be interconnected without limits* is closely linked to unlimited storage. This enables internally available information to be linked with external information fragments from, for example, the web, social media, or knowledge databases. Fast networks, as well as easy-to-use and standardized access protocols and APIs form the technical basis. This works even if there is no unambiguous key information available for linking independent datasets. Intelligent algorithms that match, often work heuristically and are often good enough to create connections. The phenomenon of unlimited networking implies that application systems can have an infinite information base at their disposal—even if this information has not been self-generated. Networking will also benefit from a massive price reduction for information. Thus, a significant volume of "general purpose" information is presently available free of charge and it can be accessed efficiently. These include, for example, the above-mentioned geo-services, online encyclopedias, and search engines.

Information processing will, exactly as storage, be *unlimited*. Processing power will be available to virtually any extent, at any time, and in any location, because microprocessors are becoming more powerful and, at the same time, cheaper—and cloud services are simplifying the use of processing capacity. Furthermore, connectivity will enable the availability of processing power at any location. Even micro-devices—due to their connection to large IT infrastructures—will have a performance capability that today's mainframe computers cannot match. In addition, the phenomenon of architectures becoming increasingly distributed, as well as the unlimited linking of information outlined above, also implies that the processing capacities of external infrastructures can be used (possibly free of charge). If, for example, search queries are carried out via Google, Google's processing capacity is used for this purpose and it does not have to be maintained by the user. This development enables data analysis and calculations of previously unimaginable dimensions—with the potential to develop intelligent systems based on large-scale distributed infrastructures.

Last but not least, it is foreseeable that *the operation of digital machines will be unlimited*. Nowadays there are already very capable robots—they differ from "simple" computers in that they have actuators and can thus influence their physical environment. We presume that the number of actuators will increase drastically. This will be evident in a large number of specialized, but also general-purpose robots, which will initially be able to perform simple—and then increasingly complex—tasks autonomously [4].

The unlimited processing of information and knowledge has far-reaching consequences. The combined effect of the developments outlined above has vast potential for companies. In future, it will be possible (a) to represent reality (almost) completely virtually, (b) to solve any problems on this basis by using complex heuristics that operate with this information, and (c) to influence our physical environment by means of actuators. It will be possible to develop intelligent computer systems and robots that know more, make better decisions, and act more reliably than humans. In addition, future systems will also have the capacity to learn faster and better than humans. On the one hand, this opens up completely new areas of application and application scenarios for information technology. On the other hand, this raises many ethical, economic, and socio-political questions that need to be asked, discussed, and answered. In order to illustrate the technology potential, certain selected applications are presented in more detail below. A few of these are future projections that are not (yet) reality. In some of the cases, however, such developments and technologies can already be observed today. We base our presentation on core operational functions to emphasize that the trends shown here are relevant for all corporate divisions. We obviously do not claim that the information provided is complete. Importantly, many examples are considered critical, due to data protection and ethical considerations. We do not, however, deal separately with the possible legal restrictions of the presented procedures. On the one hand, it is completely unclear in which direction the socio-political debate and legislation will develop concerning these problems. On the other hand, there are, for example, countries that are not remotely as rigorous as Germany when it comes to protecting privacy and processing personal data. It is interesting that, especially in Germany, two opposing developments are noticeable: The topic of data security and data protection is, on the one hand, often the subject of heated socio-political debate, which indicates a particular high level of awareness. This, on the other hand, does not prevent millions of private social media users from giving the general public access to comprehensive details of their private lives. These data are largely unprotected and already available to companies and other organizations for automated evaluation.

Digitalization in Marketing and Sales

The marketing and sales functions—especially in companies that offer products and services to end customers—were already subjected to digitalization initiatives at an early stage. One logical step is to collect information about customers to better understand them and to make better offers available to them. It is therefore obvious that companies are already trying to complete their customer profile to a very large extent by generating customer-related data. This includes, for example, using data from social media such as online contributions, videos and photos (including geotagging), user interaction, and also individual networks [5]. For this purpose, companies either use freely accessible user data, or create interaction spaces through their own social media presence and activities. They can also analyze web logs and surf profiles. Specialized companies in the advertising industry use cookies and advanced techniques to monitor users across different websites and analyze their browsing behavior. Large providers of free Internet services (such as Google or Yahoo) have a wide range of user information that is made available, directly or indirectly, to interested companies. Large online retailers (such as Amazon) also generate significant amounts of their own user data, which can also be accessed. It is noteworthy that leading online companies such as Google can use a diversified range of services to collect and link very diverse information about their customers. This includes not only browsing profiles or activities in social media, but also motion profiles or user-created documents for private or professional use. New sensors in mobile devices or clothing generate even more data. Video streaming in the retail sector already enables customers to be identified in real time in certain locations—without the need for a vigilant salesperson.

Much of these data are not stored directly in the data processing centers of companies that sell products and services. Instead, data are in the domain of the Internet-based advertising industry, which indirectly make data available, namely by submitting certain goods and services depending on consumer characteristics. Here, Google's advertising services can serve as an example. The same applies to other freely available user-related data from the Internet—in many cases, storage on the servers of the user company is not even necessary. Selective searches are carried out and only data of interest are stored (if at all) locally. Then, the particular challenge is to relate own customer-related data, such as customer number and name, to the freely available customer data on the Internet. Such mapping can occur in different ways by using, for example, addresses or credit card information. If the information is linked successfully, there are virtually no technical limits to the enrichment of customers' master data: Motion profiles, activity profiles, participation in events and happenings, meetings with friends and family—all this and more can be automatically derived from existing data pools, provided there are no restrictions imposed by law or the user. It is also possible to increasingly interpret elements of such (almost) complete user profiles semantically, for example, by linking elements of the profile with semantically enriched knowledge resources. At present, Google is already operating this successfully.

According to the developments outlined above, it is self-evident that the collection of customer-related data does not stop there. Researchers are already working on heuristic algorithms that are supposed to bestow intelligence on the future marketing and sales systems. It is thus possible to draw conclusions on the basis of social media data regarding political orientations, socio-economic status, emotional state, aesthetic preferences, value systems, or consumer characteristics [6]. This data can be used to make purchase and service offers with a high probability of acceptance. It can reach a point where the emotional state—depending on the time of day, events in the daily routine, and social interactions—are analyzed to approach the buyer in a moment of "weakness" or a particular propensity to buy. In principle, the communication itself can occur on any sales channel, for example, directly via apps on mobile devices, in the social media, in shops, or also by e-mail. This profiling is already happening, but its full potential will only be exploited in the years ahead.

These new marketing and sales approaches have far-reaching implications. On an individual level, we identify a "transparent consumer", at least in certain areas. This phenomenon enables an unprecedented form of 1:1 marketing [7] in which companies can understand consumers better than they understand themselves—all-encompassing and in real time [8, 9]. This can dramatically increase sales success—it is largely automated and comes at a comparatively low cost. Customer loyalty can also be strengthened in the long term, because the customer feels fully understood. But he is also subjected to a subtle and probably incomprehensible influence. This has ethical implications which need to be resolved in a socio-political debate. We do not, however, expect that this trend can be fundamentally prevented. The question will be whether the buyer can still control these processes?

At the corporate and market level, the new technology has the potential to track and even forecast new trends and fashions by analyzing customer data in real time. This means that new products and services can be designed, produced, and offered to the point. Non-sellers will, more and more, become a thing of the past. These forecasts also enable better management of supply chains. Companies will also be capable of initiating and steering trends, as well as fashions, even more actively—in a subtle way that is no longer obvious to most consumers.

This is a revolution; many marketing models and concepts have to be questioned or even rejected in view of these developments. For example, the communication and pricing policies of many companies are changing fundamentally. Retailers are already exploring the possibility of setting prices according to the time of day. For example, foodstuffs become more expensive during peak periods and cheaper during off-peak periods [10]. Until then, however, the current systems will have to undergo significantly further development. Among other things, customer relationship management systems (CRM systems) will be expanded to include appropriate intelligent procedures, as well as connections to social media, the point of sale (POS), or relevant resources from the web.

Digitalization in Purchasing

The purchasing function of companies is undergoing a similar change. Nowadays, procurement processes are already automated to a very large extent, especially through the use of integrated enterprise resource planning (ERP) systems. In future, however, purchasing will again change significantly—beyond automation. A key driver of this change is that it will become increasingly easier in future to collect or generate information that is relevant to purchasing. For example, with sensors on raw materials and commodities, or on their packaging and containers, it will be possible to measure the consumption thereof. It will similarly be possible to record motion (for example, from the warehouse to the production site). Fundamentally, this is nothing new and has been known for decades under the keyword production data acquisition. However, it will be possible to record such activities in real time, without the intervention of people, and with unprecedented accuracy. It will even be possible to record service provision status. For example, it is conceivable that a room's degree of cleanliness (e.g., cleanliness of heavily frequented toilet facilities) can be automatically detected and then, if necessary, cleaning services can be requested. It will also be easier to collect information about (potential) suppliers and service providers. Experience reports, annual reports, stock market information, press releases, product and service information, as well as other information, are often freely available on the Internet. They can be analyzed without the need for long-term data storage. These resources are, instead, searched for as needed on the web, linked to internal supplier data, and thus made available for evaluations. Intelligent algorithms can use consumption information to predict requirements, identify suitable suppliers, and create order proposals. In the case of non-critical requirements, it is also conceivable that the systems will have the ability to place autonomous purchase orders; no dispatcher will then be required. With such a "just-in-time predictive procurement," order processes will be planned and carried out such that inventories are automatically minimized [11].

It is easy to imagine that important suppliers, in particular, are automatically subjected to a 360-degree evaluation. External information (see above) and internal information (e.g., from internal social media and purchasing systems) are used to comprehensively assess the quality and performance of suppliers. Information about complaints, problem cases, or breached delivery commitments are integrated, entirely automatically, into the analysis. Such "intelligent performance assessments" would then enable a possible forecast of the supplier's or service provider's future willingness and performance—without the need for buyers to become active. This prevents delivery and performance failures; it also ensures consistently high quality. It also simplifies the management of a future-oriented supplier portfolio considerably.

Digitalization in Logistics

Digitalization will have particularly noticeable consequences for logistics. The completely digital recording of goods flows is already becoming noticeable. This enables real-time information about the whereabouts and status of each individual shipment and applies to both intra- and inter-organizational logistics processes, such as those for warehouses, production lines, and delivery routes. The necessary technology is already partially available. In this context, the keywords are: global positioning system (GPS), radio frequency identification (RFID), or near field communication (NFC). Furthermore, there is also video surveillance, the use of wireless networks such as WLAN or LTE, and increasingly intelligent packaging, which stores information about the goods to be transported and which records the status of the goods with the aid of sensors. For example, in this way the foodstuff temperature can be recorded, or it is possible to determine whether the goods are spoiled.

Apart from recording individual transport movements, the entire volume of traffic will also be logged in detail. Each individual road user will be capable of reporting position, movement and, if necessary, destination data. In addition, cameras, satellites, and other sensors record traffic and thus also register road users who do not provide their own position data. Information about the weather and special events are also relevant for logistical purposes. The latter include, for example, construction sites, roadblocks, accidents, and major events that can have a significant impact on traffic volume and flow.

Much of the information outlined above is not stored centrally by the owner of the goods or the road users, but rather through decentralized storage or by external service providers. Logistics service providers already offer data tracking for the delivery of goods. Traffic information and weather data can also be retrieved from external providers as required. We therefore predict a widespread distribution of information systems in the logistics sector, based on the fact that various data sources will be interconnected across organizational boundaries. Intelligent systems, which are equipped with text recognition algorithms, can identify major events by analyzing social media and include them in traffic forecasts. It is also conceivable that individual personal data from social media will be analyzed and aggregated to estimate the expected traffic volume. If, for example, many posts refer to the fact that, because of the good weather, it is a good idea to plan a trip to the lake, it can be concluded from this that the access roads will in all likelihood be congested, due to the high volume of traffic. This means that practically complete traffic information is available, which enables very reliable short, medium, and long-term forecasts. Although the calculations of these are complex and time-consuming, they can easily be made available in unlimited cloud structures.

"Predicted traffic" will enable considerably more reliable logistics at the micro-level, which will make just-in-time deliveries much easier, even for high-risk traffic routes. This prevents production downtime or high stock levels. A seamless link to production planning and control systems (PPS) further increases the benefits. If these technologies are combined with driverless transport systems, which are already available (e.g., self-driving cars, trucks, ships, or trains), it is conceivable that the logistics of the future will be almost completely automated. Breaks, sick leave, and holidays will become less important. Humans will only need to intervene in exceptional cases. At the same time, deliveries become cheaper, faster, and more punctual. Furthermore, the quality of goods will be less affected.

At a macro level, it is imaginable that traffic systems will be controlled such that congestion, delays, or accidents are largely avoided. The triad of driverless transport systems, the complete networking of road users, and complete traffic information are the basis for central monitoring and control systems that control traffic flows in advance and in real time. In certain areas, they also automatically reconcile the supply of and demand for transport capacity. Perhaps at some point in time using the motorway during rush hour will be more expensive than using it during non-productive hours—such a monetary control will be implemented. It is also conceivable that perishable goods will have priority and that express goods will be allowed to use special "fast lanes." At the same time, the safety of the transport systems will continue to increase. Whether such a control system is implemented as "swarm intelligence" (e.g., in the case of the automobile), or whether it is implemented by a central system (e.g., in the railway context) is probably of secondary importance for the final result.

These changes have significant consequences. On the one hand, considerable improvements in transport handling are expected, which is likely to have a positive impact on the economy. On the other hand, however, massive job cuts are expected because many of the logistics sub-tasks will have to be rationalized and automated in future. This even applies to the tasks that currently still require the intelligence, experience, and foresighted planning of a dispatcher.

Digitalization in Production

Production will also encounter a multiplication of generated information. Machines and robots are increasingly equipped with sensors that record information about the environment, the work task, the progress of work, and internal conditions. The number of sensors is currently growing exponentially in many areas. We cannot yet predict when this trend will slow down. Logistical data (see above) are added via newly introduced or handed-down work tasks or end products. This information is collected and partly stored in central production planning and control systems, and partly also in local autonomous production facilities. Due to interconnectedness, they can easily be shared or transmitted along the production chain. In certain cases, the parts themselves will also carry this information. The production plants', machines', and robots' degree of interconnectedness will increase significantly. All systems, objects, and actors involved in production such as control consoles, customer and supplier systems, the products themselves, or logistics systems will have the ability to send and receive information. This means that it will be technically possible to coordinate production processes proactively and predictively. The machines and robots, which are involved in the production process, can, for example, also learn how to minimize waste and spoilage, or to recognize when maintenance is required. We will therefore be dealing with robots that are capable of handling a certain level of introspection and, thus, autonomously control the production process. The seamless information flow, as well as the flexibility of the machines, will also enable parts to be machined individually, that is, on a batch size of one basis. For this purpose, machines and robots will automatically program or configure themselves if necessary and, for example, handle the necessary tools autonomously. The machines will, thus, adapt to changing requirements without human intervention. If this possibility is linked to the progress made in marketing (see above), it will enable the production of individual products (possibly even anticipatory) according to consumer needs. Due to the machines' flexibility, their capacity will also be increased. It is also conceivable that the production capacities at other production sites will be temporarily changed if one's own possibilities are not sufficient. This happens without much planning effort and occurs, largely autonomously, through intelligent production and logistics systems. This results in an economic and ecological benefit, because scarce production capacities are used to the best possible extent. In this way, inventories are further reduced, production and delivery times are shortened, and a higher customer orientation is realized. Ultimately, production gains "elasticity."

Digitalization in Human Resource Management

Digitalization will also fundamentally change the human resource (HR) function in companies. It will become increasingly easier to generate and collect comprehensive information about potential and current employees. Particularly the internal and external social media used by (potential) employees offer a rich pool of data. Social networks such as Xing, LinkedIn, Facebook, as well as blogs and discussion forums make it possible to draw conclusions about personality traits, attitudes, hobbies and other activities [12]. As it will be possible to create the transparent customer (see above), so will it also be possible to create the transparent employee. Here, too, the relevant data does not have to be stored entirely in the company's own IT infrastructure. On the contrary, it will be possible to carry out automatic searches, if required, and the results will then be saved locally if necessary. Since it is generally not possible to use unique identifying characteristics, such as a personnel number (they are only used internally), an external search must operate with characteristic bundles. This means that the relevant person is searched by, for example, using his name and place of residence. Gender, the (approximate) age, or other external characteristics can also help identify a person in social media. Text and image recognition methods will make it relatively easy to evaluate the corresponding information in future. The situation is much simpler with internal social media. Here, a mapping of user names or user IDs can be used to easily establish a connection to personnel master data. In most cases, this mapping will be saved permanently.

As is the case with the customer, the available information can be used to draw a wide range of conclusions that can be relevant for performance measurement, as well as staff development or deployment. Under the catchphrase "social media mining," very powerful algorithms are being developed that can draw far-reaching conclusions from large amounts of unstructured data. It will therefore be easy to find out how healthy an employee is, how high his or her failure risk is, what level of salary is appropriate, whether the employee represents the company appropriately, whether he or she is working hard, is emotionally balanced, or even has psychological problems.

The effects are far-reaching: Applicants can be subjected to an automatic pre-screening, whereby the application documents are also automatically analyzed. Companies can develop a very deep understanding of their employees and can accurately design personnel development measures. Potential assessments, for example with regard to the next generation of managers, are also conceivable. For all these application areas, existing HR systems must be equipped with correspondingly new intelligent functions, as well as access to social media and additional information sources.

Digitalization in Finance and Controlling

Last but not least, digitalization will have a significant impact on a company's financial function. A study by Accenture, a US management consultancy, predicts a total disruption of finance departments which, according to the authors, will—compared to the present—have a completely different look in the leading companies as early as 2020 [13]. These changes particularly affect the controlling area, which is already very involved in supplying the company with decision-relevant information. Exactly here, is an enormous need for improvement and therefore the new digital technologies such as big data analytics, cloud computing, and intelligent systems are perfectly positioned.

Predictive forecasting is credited with a significant role in the transformation process. Essentially, this involves that proactive-prognostic approaches replace the reactive-analytical evaluation of historical data; we expect this to be significantly more accurate than traditional predictions [14]. At present, forecasting processes are still operated manually and with great effort in most companies. Moreover, they are often criticized for being politically motivated. Using big data and predictive analytics now makes it possible to automatically generate forecasts from granular data. Through an application of stochastic models, machine learning, and data mining approaches, such forecasts will not only become more efficient; it will also lead to significantly better results.

Generally, "digital corporate management" will benefit from the fact that, in future, control cycles and optimizations will be agile and will occur in real time. Automated analyses will shorten response times, enable "high-frequency decisions," and lead to the ongoing identification of possible optimization measures. The new digital approaches enable automatically made—and therefore faster—decisions within defined value and risk limits, based on the probabilities of forecast results. As digitalization will lead to even stronger cross-company networking, where information will be shared across organizational boundaries, so processes will increasingly be integrated across companies and in a way that adds value [15].

The above-mentioned changes will also impact on the organizational structure of the financial function. At this stage, we expect a stronger shift of core functions from financial departments to the various divisions—in other words, a decentralization of today's financial functions. As a result of the new technological possibilities, the various departments can directly perform traditional accounting and data preparation tasks by using automated "robotic solutions." The classic finance function itself will, however, probably develop into a central analysis unit for strategic decision support. The importance of the finance departments will therefore, in all likelihood increase fundamentally. The corresponding teams will, however, be smaller and more heterogeneous than they are at present. On the personnel side, we observe that less business economists will dominate the image of finance departments, which will increasingly be characterized by data scientists, statisticians, behavioral researchers, and possibly even anthropologists [13].

Transformation Towards a Future IT Department

In principle, many of the digital application scenarios outlined above can already be implemented, because the hardware and software with the necessary performance capabilities are available. At present, however, the above-mentioned software and hardware are not standard issue. For this reason, considerable implementation, configuration, integration, and testing efforts are required before systems can be used. In many instances, the hardware costs are also still prohibitively high. That is why many possibilities that are already conceivable, are not yet economically feasible. This particularly applies to small and medium-sized enterprises.

Our recommendation is, therefore, to closely monitor the market for the relevant technologies and products, and to assess the corresponding progress made with development. A market entry is only worthwhile if the product has reached the necessary level of maturity. Many companies consider a first mover strategy as not being worthwhile, because its costs can be too high. This is different in cases where the company has the financial resources and hopes for the first mover strategy to bring about immediate competitive advantages. Here, it can make sense to use the first mover strategy as a driving force and to gain a head start. This technology scouting should be carried out in close cooperation with the relevant department on the business side, since this is the only way to correctly assess the potential of digitalization.

It is also our considered opinion that it makes sense to combine technology scouting with domain-oriented architecture management. Specialist domains such as human resources, finance, or production are planned separately and on a long-term basis, whereby interfaces are, of course, also taken into account. One should observe digitalization trends separately for each domain and discuss how new technologies and processes can be integrated into the existing architecture. This enables one to anticipate, at an early stage, which architectural developments are necessary to prepare for changes resulting from digitalization. The results are corresponding road maps for digitalization, which also serve as a basis for investment program and portfolio planning. It is important to ensure that domain planning integrates seamlessly into a coherent overall architecture. A company architect will perform the corresponding planning and control tasks. Domain planning should also be part of the company's medium- and long-term digital strategy. New digital products and services, or new business models, usually place multiple demands on the company's various functional areas. At this stage it is already clear that the future IT function will have to take on new tasks: It is, therefore, necessary to identify potential innovations at an early stage so that they can be transformed into operational systems, products, services, or business models, in accordance with strategic considerations.

Overview: No Business Without IT
- The new technological possibilities of digitalization significantly exceed previous waves of innovation.
- Digital transformation is based on *virtually unlimited* possibilities to generate, store, network, and process information.
- A further new feature is that intelligent machines can now directly influence their physical environment (actuators).
- This will enable machines to perform even more complex planning or controlling tasks.
- Machines will operate more reliably and better than humans—initially, in clearly defined areas, but then also in more wide-ranging ones.
- Digitalization affects almost all areas of the company.
- In many cases, current value creation processes and practices are being revolutionized.

References

1. Bower, J. L., & Christensen, C. M. (1995). Disruptive technologies. Catching the wave. *Harvard Business Review, 69*, 19–45.
2. Rolls Royce. (2016). *Engine health management*. http://www.rolls-royce.com/about/our-tech nology/enabling-technologies/engine-health-management.aspx
3. Mosco, V. (2014). *To the cloud—Big data in a turbulent world*. New York: Taylor & Francis.
4. Ford, M. (2016). *Rise of the robots—Technology and the threat of mass unemployment*. Philadelphia: Basic Books.
5. Russell, M. A. (2013). *Mining the social web*. Cambridge: O'Reilly.
6. Thelwall, M., Wilkinson, D., & Uppal, S. (2009). Data mining emotion in social network communication—Gender differences in MySpace. *Journal of the American Society for Information Science and Technology, 61*, 190–199.
7. Peppers, D., & Roger, M. (1997). *The one to one future*. New York: Currency Doubleday.
8. Agresta, S., & Bough, B. B. (2011). *Perspectives on social media marketing*. Boston: Cengage Learning.

9. Moutinho, L., Bigné, E., & Manrai, A. K. (2014). *The Routledge companion to the future of marketing*. New York: Routledge.
10. The Huffington Post. (2014, August 26). Elektronische Preisschilder: Rewe kann bald die Preise sekündlich ändern. http://www.huffingtonpost.de/2014/08/26/rewe-elektronische-preisschilder_n_5714583.html
11. Lamoureux, M. (2014). Procurement trend #6—Data-based predictive analytics. *Sourcing Innovation*. http://sourcinginnovation.com/wordpress/2014/12/11/procurement-trend-06-data-based-predictive-analytics/
12. Spitzer, B., Vernet, A. K., Sonderstorm, C., & Narnbiar, R. (2013). *Using digital tools to unlock HR's true potential*. Paris: Capgemini.
13. Hedtstück, M. (2015, November 12). Bis spätestens 2020: Accenture prophezeit totale Disruption der Finanzfunktion. *Finance Magazin*. http://www.finance-magazin.de/bilanzierung-controlling/finanzplanung/accenture-prophezeit-totale-disruption-der-finanzfunktion-1367601/
14. Mehanna, W., Müller, F., & Tunco, C. (2015a). Predictive Forecasting und did Digitalisierung der Unternehmenssteuerung, IM+io Fachzeitschrift für Innovation. *Organisation und Management* (Heft 4), 28–32.
15. Mehanna, W., Tobias, S., & Zierhofer, R. (2015b). *Die neue Welt der Unternehmenssteuerung*. The Performance Architect 2/2015, pp. 8–12.

Development and Operation Are Not Decisive: IT Management Follows the "Innovate-Design-Transform" Paradigm

Ever since its inception, information technology has been viewed as a means of automating and rationalizing business processes. Unsurprisingly, in the years of its development, corporate IT has developed ever more professional structures and processes to accommodate the needs of business departments, plan appropriate IT support, implement them, and then operate and offer them in the form of IT services. IT departments often work in a reactive way, that is, they "wait" for the wishes of the business departments. They are thus usually perceived as internal company support functions or service providers.

However, due to the current digitalization trend, many IT departments face much more far-reaching requirements. In view of current developments, it is crucial for many companies to generate business and value-added innovations effectively and efficiently; it is also crucial for many companies to develop appropriate IT solutions and to realign their company to remain competitive (see chapter "No business without IT: IT is the central and indispensable driver of entrepreneurial value creation"). The affected IT departments are challenged to participate proactively and to guide the required IT changes. At present, however, the majority of IT departments are not yet fulfilling this role, since—as reactive service providers—they do not have the structures, processes, or skills to systematically develop (business) innovations. In addition, IT departments are often perceived as bureaucratic, inflexible, and not on an equal footing with the business departments. For example, according to the business departments the short-term changes to information systems are not implemented quickly enough when the IT department decides to commit to certain time frames to implement those changes.

Against this background, the question arises how IT departments can strategically develop into an innovation partner within their company. To this end, we discuss the weaknesses of the currently very established *plan-build-run* paradigm and present a new IT management paradigm, which we call *innovate-design-transform* [1]. We also explain the specific competencies IT departments—that follow this paradigm—must develop to face the digital transformation.

© Springer International Publishing AG, part of Springer Nature 2019   41
N. Urbach, F. Ahlemann, *IT Management in the Digital Age*, Management for Professionals, https://doi.org/10.1007/978-3-319-96187-3_4

The Development Towards Industrialized IT Management

IT management underwent a major change in recent years. Initially, it was primarily a matter of speeding up computer-intensive routine tasks when using IT, but it soon became clear that there is more potential in the integrated support of complete business processes. In this context, enterprise resource planning (ERP), supply chain management (SCM), and customer relationship management (CRM) systems were developed. This enabled efficient processes on the one hand, and better decision-making support for management on the other. This, however, required substantial investments and major projects. In view of the increasing IT investment and the companies' growing dependency on IT, it was only natural for companies to systematically *plan* and *build* new technologies, and *run* the resulting services efficiently. To date, the majority of IT departments have used this approach (*plan-build-run*).

Against the background of developments such as IT outsourcing and application service providing (ASP), it soon became clear in many companies that *plan-build-run* no longer adequately reflected the IT department's reality. Instead of carrying out extensive system planning and implementation by themselves, more and more companies shortened their IT value chain by handing over portions of this chain to external partners. Outsourced IT service desks or leased hardware, including the associated maintenance by external partners, exemplify this. As a result, many IT departments experienced a similar trend than the one in the manufacturing industry that led to the development of supply chain management and corresponding reference models. In the mid-2000s, the *plan-build-run* paradigm was therefore further developed into an integrated information management model (IIM model). This new approach encompasses the following phases: resource procurement and supplier management (source), coordinating the service production process (make), as well as managing customer relationships, recording customer requirements, and the operative control of the customer interface (delivery) [2].

Plan-build-run and *source-make-deliver* both emphasize the independence of the IT value chain, which requires—to a large extent—independent planning and control. It is monitored by specialists who communicate with (usually internal) customers via clearly defined interfaces. This facilitates outsourcing portions of the value chain, thereby making the IT department at least partially replaceable. In light of this, IT management focuses on efficiency and reliability. IT services are created and operated by using processes that resemble highly automated assembly line manufacturing. The central goals are cost efficiency, reliability, and high-quality processes. However, at present many companies face the challenges of digitalization: Disruptive, IT-based innovations jeopardize established business and value creation models and require adequate solutions and proactive action.

Industrialized IT Management Reaches Its Limits

Many companies' IT departments still only provide IT infrastructure services and the subsequent application systems. In addition, there are accompanying services such as the IT helpdesk and services related to IT projects. It is doubtful whether such an arrangement is sufficient to play a driving role in the digitalization of business and value creation models. In future, the central challenge to IT management will be to help develop and implement the innovations outlined above, and steer or even drive the necessary organizational changes within the company. It is necessary to draw attention to aspects that IT managers previously rarely encountered: How can the IT department (co-)develop new business and value creation models based on new technologies? What data is available to the company or can be generated, and what conclusions can be drawn from it? Which technological innovations can be expected and what potential do they have? Although companies presently only have access to very few concrete solutions that provide an easy answer to these and other questions, it is clear that the existing IT management paradigms *plan-build-run* and *source-make-deliver* only meet the new challenges to a limited extent.

Due to complex planning phases, the *plan-build-run* paradigm leads to relatively long time-to-market times, which become challenging with fast innovation cycles. Classic IT planning is too rigid for reacting to market and technology trends in a reasonable time. In the development phase, IT departments occasionally develop their own solutions and do not bundle their resources in a sufficient form. In addition, *plan-build-run* emphasizes the efficient management of the IT value chain and ignores short-term, external, market-oriented, or technological impulses. Furthermore, IT departments that follow the plan-build-run paradigm have structures that promote the development of IT skills, but these structures rarely lead to an accumulation of industry or business model know-how, or (deep) business process know-how.

The focus on in-house development has given way to the *source-make-deliver* paradigm, which creates a broader reference context. It has a stronger focus on supplier and customer relationships for procuring and providing services or other resources; thereby giving the IT department access to intensively use partner networks. The integration of partners can mean a further increase in an IT department's efficiency, because each partner can concentrate on its core competence. This paradigm is thus also geared for process efficiency. Accordingly, the same applies here: The paradigm is not suitable for incorporating external impulses based on far-reaching business know-how and then launching corresponding innovations.

Requirements from a New IT Management Paradigm

Neither the business departments, nor the IT department can master the challenges of digitalization in isolation of each other. In the digital age, we believe there are three key demands on the future IT department that will require its transformation.

First of all, the IT department's ability to innovate must become more agile. Thereby, the department gains more flexibility and can respond to market events in a reasonable time. Here, the first steps would, for example, be rolling planning and more flexible budgets to ensure that innovations are implemented and advanced faster. There is also a need for partnership-based and customer-oriented models of cooperation and innovation development.

The future IT departments should also focus less on the creation and development, but rather, on the *ability to design* the right solution for a specific operational purpose. The solution concept should always be conceived and designed from the customer's point of view and can also be carried out in collaboration with partner networks. As a result of increasingly open cooperation, innovative approaches are turned into solution designs that are further developed and prepared for operational use. A new paradigm should therefore also consider design-thinking approaches [3] to enable the conception and operationalization of innovative products and services geared for users' needs. The actual implementation of the innovation in terms of technology development, configuration, or integration can often be carried out by external partners. However, it is necessary to keep in mind that the developed designs can be seamlessly integrated into the company architecture, which requires dedicated architecture management.

The dynamics of the developments in digitalization put constant pressure on companies to change. The companies, and especially their IT departments, will need to drive and implement the changes quickly and reliably. This requires an extensive *capability to transform*. Following the design and subsequent implementation of innovations in the context of business and value creation models, the company, as well as its structures and processes, must be changed accordingly. However, many companies are characterized by a high degree of persistence. Change management is therefore one of the most important requirements from a future paradigm. This new paradigm means that the IT department's role will change from being a service provider to being an innovation partner on an equal footing.

The New Paradigm: Innovate-Design-Transform

The above challenges of the digitalization era require that the IT department is realigned to meet the demands of innovation, design, and transformation. We propose a new paradigm aimed at meeting these three central requirements.

Targeted innovation development (*innovate*) is the first phase of the new paradigm. Above all else, it requires efforts with regard to strategic objectives and corresponding budgets, collaboration with customers and partners, stringent processes of innovation management, as well as individual freedom and an innovation culture. IT-related innovation activities should follow clear innovation objectives anchored in the digital strategy. In the absence of such a strategic anchoring, it will be difficult to set the necessary priorities, communicate innovation activities to employees, guide them in a targeted way, and measure the success of the innovation activities. However, unlike traditional IT management paradigms that focused on optimizing internal IT processes, innovation will focus on (internal and external) customers and business partners. If not, digitalized business and value creation models will not be (further) developed. It is clearly not sufficient to merely set targets. The future IT department must have the financial resources to drive innovation. IT departments should therefore have a dedicated innovation budget. Since innovation activity is directed at the outside world, collaborations with customers and business partners also require new cooperation models. Thus far, the interfaces between IT and specialist business departments in many companies have been formalized and are contractually regulated. For example, the parties use service level agreements (SLAs), which specify the customer's rights and the IT department's duties. IT departments often have a language and culture that differ from their customers', and therefore communication becomes even more difficult. It is questionable whether such interfaces can lead to a trustful, creative, flexible, and future-oriented cooperation. Current IT departments must therefore ask themselves how to collaborate with customers in future. At the same time, it may, for example, be necessary to integrate external partners into innovation projects to compensate for competence shortfalls and gain external impulses. Such open innovation activities can improve innovation success in a sustainable way. For example, customers and suppliers can actively participate in developing new products and services and express their wishes via a dedicated platform. Not every innovation idea will be implemented. As a rule, a large number of innovation ideas are generated and tested, and only the most promising ones are followed up. An (open) innovation management process must be established to keep track of an IT department's innovation activities and to be able to prioritize and control these in a targeted manner. This should include a review of the feasibility of ideas and their financial assessment. In particular, this can help understand which activities affect innovation success, especially when it comes to the expansion of innovation activities and increased cooperation between companies from different sectors. In order to create collective work and innovation, the IT department needs to have freedom. Only employees who are able to deal with business developments and technologies can creatively and proactively produce the innovations described above. There is also a need for interdisciplinary teams that draw together different educational backgrounds, experience, and skills. A climate that encourages innovation in IT departments—allowing for collaboration and freedom—is just as necessary as innovation-oriented incentive systems. For example, an organization should be able to cope with the fact that innovation projects are discontinued because, contrary to expectations, there is no sign of market potential. It should be interpreted as a learning experience and not as a failure.

As soon as concepts for the innovation of business and value creation models are developed, they must be implemented. The detailed functional and technical specifications (*design*) play a crucial role as the basis for subsequent development. It is noticeable that (especially young) IT users are less and less willing to accept compromises in the area of user interface design. In many cases, the experience in dealing with end devices and applications for consumers is transferred to business information systems. Users expect similar user-friendliness that requires (almost) no training, as well as continuous development and improvement of systems at short intervals. Similarly, the intensity of competition in many industries requires that new solutions are developed quickly. For these reasons, it is crucial for companies to be able to quickly develop functional systems that enjoy a high level of user acceptance. Whereas the design of IT solutions plays a central role, software development itself is becoming less important. Here, specialized service providers are available who, although they often do not have the necessary industry know-how and innovation competence outlined above, can implement solutions efficiently and cost-effectively, due to specific technology knowledge and project experience based on precise specifications. This technology and project expertise can often be better developed and maintained by external operators, because they can achieve economies of scale by working with a variety of customers. Many companies find it, therefore, less and less attractive to have resources available for the technical implementation of innovative IT solutions. In future, design competence will be decisive for success—more than ever before. In order to successfully complete the design process, the following will be required: interdisciplinary teams involving partners, agile project management principles and design thinking approaches, as well as the early involvement of future development partners. Interdisciplinary teams should be involved in the design of innovative, customer-oriented IT solutions, because technical expertise from different areas will be necessary. In the majority of cases, profound market knowledge, technological know-how, knowledge of the company architecture, business process knowledge, and project management skills are required. Since this knowledge is often not fully available in the company, partner networks should, thus, be used for collaboration to develop integrated and coordinated solutions. The process of developing solutions can be enriched by the design-thinking method, which was developed for solving complex design questions in interdisciplinary teams [4]. Agile project management principles must also be considered. In this way, solutions can be implemented faster, thereby increasing the value contribution. The developers should be involved as early as possible in the design process to avoid situations in which the later development partner or the own developers do not understand the solution and its objectives. This is indispensable, especially if you want to work according to flexible project management principles in terms whereof design and implementation phases overlap.

As a last step, the various business areas and IT department needs to adapt the implementation of the previously conceived IT solutions, which, due to their far-reaching nature, are called transformations (*transform*). New business models can require completely new organizational structures and processes in the sales, service, and logistics areas. In order to carry out such transformations successfully, implementation projects or programs, governance structures and controlling systems, as well as comprehensive change management in the business units are required. The IT department must, first of all, ensure that the IT solutions are technically implemented, which is usually carried out in the context of a project. The entire company architecture must be considered. This means that a seamless integration into the existing IT infrastructure and application landscape has to be achieved. At the same time, it should be noted that operational, maintenance, and support processes may need adjustments. For example, it may be necessary to establish a requirements management process, or adapt the existing one, so that new solutions can be fully integrated and controlled from the customer's request to the final handover to the customer. These changes often require the targeted development of specific knowledge and skills among employees, which can be realized through appropriate training and further education. In addition, it may also be necessary to change governance structures such that management acts in accordance with business or value creation model innovations. For example, it is important to reassess the roles and responsibilities for the adapted processes and to adjust them where necessary. Controlling systems are also important for measuring the transformation progress and the degree to which it has achieved its goals. For example, key figures in the area of requirements management can provide information on the time that certain process stages take, or on the costs that were incurred for changing the requirements. On the business departments' side, the planned business and value creation model innovations must be implemented simultaneously. This will lead to changed business processes and organizational structures. Due to the extent of the changes, systematic change management will be necessary to "guide" the employees through the change process, since this is the only way to minimize employee resistance and ensure smooth implementation. The IT department can support these changes, because the business processes are closely linked to the required information technologies.

Capabilities of the Future IT Department

The progression of corporate IT towards an *innovate-design-transform* paradigm is not an easy process. The necessary changes are far-reaching and affect many aspects of the IT and business departments. New structures need to be created, processes need to be adapted, competencies need to be developed, and a cultural change needs to be initiated. From a scientific point of view, these changes can be understood as a process of building organizational capabilities that enable a company to differentiate itself from the competition. Such skills can only be developed in the long term, are often difficult to imitate, are hardly replaceable, and are rare. Unsurprisingly, in many industries only a few companies really know how to take advantage of the opportunities offered by digitalization and how to derive sustainable competitive advantages from it. This has the following implications for the management of the transformation: First, one must accept that the transformation process cannot be carried out in the context of a single, limited project. Instead, a long-term initiative is necessary to develop the necessary skills. Second, the transformation must not be interpreted as a purely technological initiative. Instead, it affects almost all areas of strategic and operational management. Since many cases require far-reaching changes in the value system and employee behavior, one also has to reckon with potential resistance. This emphasizes the special role of sensible change management. Third, digital transformation requires an external orientation. On the one hand, this is necessary to identify relevant market-oriented and technological developments at an early stage, and to subsequently analyze them. On the other hand, digital transformation often requires competencies and resources that, in the short or medium term, can only be contributed by experienced external partners.

IT departments find it increasingly easier to outsource non-differentiating, low friction portions of their value chain to external partners, thereby initiating a focus on competitive activities. These competitive activities result from the priorities of the IT department of the future. They concern, for example, innovation and design competence, the ability to select and manage suppliers, partners, and service providers; they also concern the ability to develop and maintain sustainable, flexible, and cost-effective company architecture. This results in a reduced focus on technical fields of activity, such as development and operation. Instead, analysis activities, creative processes, and control processes are gaining in importance. This development also coincides with cultural change.

> **Overview: Development and Operation Not Decisive**
> - During digital transformation, corporate IT is required to play a proactive role in the innovation process.
> - However, many IT departments do not yet fulfill this role, because they are often perceived as being bureaucratic, inflexible, and not on an equal footing with the business departments.
> - In the context of IT industrialization, the IT management paradigm developed from *plan-build-run* to *make-source-deliver*.
> - Industrialized IT management is reaching its limits in the digital transformation.
> - The requirements from a new IT management paradigm are the ability to innovate, design, and transform.
> - Accordingly, we propose *innovate-design-transform* as a new IT management paradigm.
> - In future, IT departments will have to develop new capabilities; development and operation are no longer crucial.

References

1. Koch, P., Ahlemann, F., & Urbach, N. (2016). Die innovative IT-Organisation in der digitalen Transformation: Von Plan-Build-Run zu Innovate-Design-Transform. In S. Helmke & M. Uebel (Eds.), *Managementorientiertes IT-controlling und IT-governance* (2nd ed., pp. 177–196). Berlin: Springer.
2. Zarnekow, R., Brenner, W., & Pilgram, U. (2006). *Integrated information management—Applying successful industrial concepts in IT*. Heidelberg: Springer.
3. Grots, A., & Pratschk, M. (2009). Design thinking—Kreativität als Methode. *Marketing Review St. Gallen, 26*(2), 18–23.
4. Hilbrecht, H., & Kempkens, O. (2013). *Design Thinking im Unternehmen—Herausforderung mit Mehrwert*. Wiesbaden: Springer Gabler.

Shadow IT as a Lived Practice: IT Innovations Are Developed in Interdisciplinary Teams Within the Business Departments

The majority of IT projects are still initiated by a company's business units and only then reactively implemented by the IT department. Due to relatively slow coordination and implementation processes, as well as long development cycles, the resulting IT solutions are often not innovative and rarely disruptive. Consequently, corporate IT is perceived as a service provider rather than a creative innovator. As a result of the increased pressure for change in digital transformation and the ever more convenient sourcing possibilities of cloud computing, the business units are becoming increasingly active with regard to IT solutions—independently and without the involvement of corporate IT. The result is the "individual data processing" or "shadow IT" phenomenon, which is viewed as problematic, specifically regarding the compliance, security, and architecture requirements. In this context, we ask ourselves whether this separation of IT and business is still appropriate in the light of digitalization. We come to the conclusion that IT innovations should ideally be created where they will be used—namely in the business departments. For this purpose, experts from all relevant areas should be involved and work together. This makes the "official shadow IT" a lived practice. In this chapter we discuss the shadow IT phenomenon and present our view on the future cooperation model between the IT department and the business units.

Shadow IT as a Reaction to (Too) Long Implementation Processes

In many companies, IT projects (except for basic infrastructure projects) are initiated primarily through proposals from the business units. This approach often results in more project ideas than the IT department can actually implement—for resource reasons—in a given period of time. They, thus, need to prioritize the project proposals. This is where IT project portfolio management comes into play—it selects project proposals according to various criteria, such as strategy contribution, amortization, or risk, which are then converted to concrete project plans. Before the

© Springer International Publishing AG, part of Springer Nature 2019   49
N. Urbach, F. Ahlemann, *IT Management in the Digital Age*, Management for Professionals, https://doi.org/10.1007/978-3-319-96187-3_5

project is implemented, a comprehensive requirements analysis is usually carried out, followed by technical implementation, as well as technical and functional tests. Depending on the project volume, the time between the idea for a project and the operational project result (time-to-market) is quite long, due to long-lasting coordination and implementation processes. Moreover, due to the traditionally strict organizational separation, problems arise in the coordination between IT and business, which negatively affect the quality of the project results. Accordingly, the resulting IT solutions are usually not very innovative, which is then blamed on the IT departments.

However, in the age of digitalization, the fast and reliable design and implementation of IT-based products and services are becoming a business-critical task. Cases in which the business units do not have confidence in the IT department's solution competence, or in which the expected implementation period is too long, or in which the IT project portfolio does not even take the presented project proposal into account, the business units take more and more independent action. This is usually triggered by growing pressure on the business units to change, due to the digital transformation. In order to ensure market success, they are forced to use digital technologies to improve their processes and launch new IT-based products, as well as services, on the market. In addition, there is the current trend towards IT consumerization. Nowadays, innovative IT solutions are often found in a private context before they are deployed in business, which is why the need and demand for the in-house use of IT innovations by users is much higher than it was just a few years ago. At the same time, developments, such as cloud computing or industry-specific process standardization, make it easier to outsource elements of the IT value chain. Managing IT infrastructures, developing new software, as well as IT operations can, thus, be entrusted comparatively easily to specialized service providers who have the necessary skills and can realize economies of scale. As a result of these developments, the "shadow IT" phenomenon arises, which is the operation of IT systems or processes within a company's business units that are detached from the official IT infrastructure and outside the IT department's control. The term "shadow IT" already implies that such an unofficial use of information systems has a rather negative connotation. However, from a company-wide perspective, shadow IT also offers opportunities [1].

Controlled Handling of Shadow IT After Weighing Opportunities and Risks

The fact that IT management is generally critical of the emergence of shadow IT and tries to prevent unofficial IT activities on the part of the business units, is not surprising. Since shadow IT, according to its definition, is operated without the IT department knowing about it, IT management has no control over it. The implemented solutions are neither technically, nor strategically, integrated into the organization's IT service management. The use of shadow IT results in technological, process-related, business, and management risks [2]. The technological risks are that, through shadow IT, untested and potentially insecure IT components, which have not been developed for a certain company context, are used in exactly that company context. Since it is not integrated into the company's IT infrastructure, data security or data protection are not guaranteed. In the event of technical breakdowns and business interruptions, the IT department cannot guarantee continued operation. The risks regarding IT and business processes are, amongst others, that shadow IT usage undermines IT architecture management and significantly reduces its effectiveness. In the case of problems on the user side, shadow IT applications are by definition not maintained by IT support, and this usually has a negative impact on user satisfaction in the medium term. The established, business-relevant processes can also no longer be monitored "end-to-end." This can particularly lead to conflicts if the affected processes violate the company's compliance rules. Last but not least, shadow IT's business and management risks entail that corporate IT can no longer fully assume responsibility for business support. As a result, it not only loses control of the IT landscape, but also some of its power in the company. In addition, recruiting employees who also have IT expertise in the business departments, can impact negatively on the overall success of the company, since these employees can no longer devote themselves—to the same extent—to their actual tasks.

However, following the long-lasting negative perception of shadow IT usage, discussions about its associated opportunities have only recently begun [3]. First of all, shadow IT's high IT innovation rate is worth mentioning. When the business units identify a benefit that can be derived from using new information technology, they introduce a flexible and agile IT solution themselves without having to undergo corporate IT's long decision-making and implementation processes. Since the business units are predominantly very task-oriented in their approach to the necessary development processes, the resulting solutions are accordingly well aligned to the internal processes. As a rule, shadow IT systems address user needs very well, and often better than the systems developed by corporate IT. For this reason, such systems, when they are working well, will in all likelihood initially lead to greater satisfaction with the general IT support, but not necessarily with the IT department.

In view of the fact that the emergence of shadow IT not only entails considerable risks, but also offers opportunities for the company, the question that arises is how this can be handled to achieve the "global maximum" for the entire company. Only a few years ago, the usual IT department approach would have been to prevent the emergence of shadow IT, as far as possible, with rigorous control mechanisms. However, due to the increased pressure for IT innovation, IT departments finds themselves in a dilemma, because of such very one-sided assessments. Strict suppression of shadow IT suffocates the innovative behavior of the business units. As a result, the IT department is perceived—to an even greater extent—as an inflexible and slower service provider, instead of a creative innovator. In addition, the business units in many companies have more power than the IT department. Therefore, despite official limitations, they will often develop and operate their own IT solutions if they think that corporate IT does not provide them with optimal support or solutions. Accordingly, IT management must take care of the balancing act between flexibility and control to find a suitable solution for its company. In order to minimize shadow IT's negative effects and realize—as many as possible—of its positive effects, it is generally recommended to "legalize" shadow IT [4, 5].

In Future, IT Innovations Will Be Created Through Close Cooperation Between Business and IT

We agree that the shadow IT phenomenon should be used, particularly in view of the new challenges that companies are facing in the digital transformation context. However, we would like to go one step further and ask why shadow IT occurs at all. One of the main reasons is obviously the "artificial" separation of IT and business. Until the era of IT industrialization, such a separation was still quite sensible (see chapter "The development of corporate IT: from the beginnings to the IT department of the future"). In its early years, corporate IT was characterized by a very high degree of technical orientation and specialization. Furthermore, there were relatively few points of contact with the specialist business units, and these were handled via highly formalized interfaces. Today, however, the business units seem to have sufficient IT know-how. This is the only explanation for the current "trend" towards shadow IT. Furthermore, information technology is already an integral part of the business areas' processes, which will be even more so in future. However, traditional IT tasks, such as IT operations, become commodity services (see chapter "Development and operation are not decisive: IT management follows the "innovate-design-transform" paradigm"). Therefore, the established separation between IT and business in the context of digital transformation appears to be at least questionable.

It is our considered opinion that IT innovations should ideally be created where they will be used—in the business departments. Accordingly, we presume that, in future, application-related IT experts will work on site, together with the users in the business units. Accordingly, IT and business will merge through close cooperation at the place where the IT will be used. The development of IT systems, as well as IT-based products and services, will be carried out in interdisciplinary teams. The downstream application support and further development will also be carried out by such mixed teams. Only the operation of basic infrastructure services will still be carried out by the classic corporate IT, as is currently the case. This makes the "official shadow IT" a lived practice. By closely interlinking IT and business, the IT department can effectively assume its role as an IT innovator and create innovative IT solutions through agile software development methods and a clear end-user focus (see chapter "Focusing on the user: development processes are agile, end-user-centered, and merged with the operation"). Such a cooperation mode can realize the full potential of shadow IT. However, this requires certain necessary conditions to minimize the associated risks. These include, among other things, controlling the security risks associated with digitalization (see chapter "Digitalization as a risk: security and business continuity management are central cross-divisional functions of the company"), developing flexible and transformable IT landscapes (see chapter "Transformable IT landscapes: IT architectures are standardized, modular, flexible, ubiquitous, elastic, cost-effective, and secure"), and establishing suitable management structures (see chapter "The end of the IT department: IT experts become part of the business departments and are coordinated by a dedicated executive responsibility").

Joint Innovation Activity Requires Rethinking

Companies in which digitalization is already well advanced, often have a corporate IT that positioned itself differently by working much more closely with the business units and that often assumes a leading role in digital transformation [6]. However, the majority of companies still have this transition phase ahead of them. At this point, we think it important to emphasize that small incremental changes are not sufficient. The joint innovation activity involving IT and business requires a new thinking and involves significant change.

This transition entails a reorganization of the affected departments, which have to position themselves organizationally according to the new division of tasks. There will certainly not be a one-size-fits-all recipe that will work equally well for all companies. However, we view the most consistent implementation of "official shadow IT" as the dissolution of boundaries between departments and the establishment of an executive "digitalization" portfolio, which will essentially concentrate on management and control tasks (see chapter "The end of the IT department: IT experts become part of the business departments and are coordinated by a dedicated executive responsibility"). As described in the previous chapter, we also consider it essential to rethink and change the paradigm. Since industrialized IT management is reaching its limits in digital transformation, corporate IT must develop new capabilities. Traditional tasks, such as software development and system operation, are becoming increasingly insignificant. According to us, the requirements of a new IT management paradigm lie primarily in the ability to innovate, design, and transform (see chapter "Development and operation are not decisive: IT management follows the "innovate-design-transform" paradigm").

But it is not only the IT department, but also the IT staff who will be affected by such a model and who has to adapt to this change. As the boundaries between business units and IT departments are becoming increasingly blurred, the importance of interface competence will become more important for employees. In this regard, it will become increasingly important for IT staff to understand and master not only the technical language, but also the business language. Pure technicians are less in demand for interdisciplinary cooperation, since the identification, conception, and design of innovative, IT-based solutions with direct business benefits are of primary importance. The technical implementation of these solutions can then be assigned to a service provider (see chapter "Infrastructure as commodity: IT infrastructure services are traded on free markets and purchased as required").

The above-mentioned organizational change entails that IT management needs to clarify the question of authority. As already explained with regard to the shadow IT risks, business departments' IT activities are usually associated with a loss of authority. Here too, a dilemma arises. On the one hand, it is not unlikely that CIOs or IT managers will lose their influence, and probably also a large part of their staff, to the business departments if the tasks of IT and business are truly merged. On the other hand, those responsible for the business departments will be given considerably more room to maneuver while simultaneously being given more IT responsibilities. Accordingly, the business units also need managers with the necessary IT know-how. However, the required employee skills are very scarce on the market and this has corresponding human resource management implications for the entire company (see chapter "Demography, digital natives, and individual entrepreneurship: employees become a strategic competitive factor").

Co-location as Transition Model for Legal Shadow IT

At this point, the question that arises is how the proposed cooperation model can be put into practice. We believe that the changes outlined above can be tackled very easily and directly, if there is a will to do so. An approach that has already been put into practice is the "co-location" organizational form, which, in our opinion, can very well serve as a transition model at this stage. This model envisages that although IT employees work "on site" at the internal business unit customers, they remain subordinate to the IT department. For example, the "embedded" employees often work as demand managers, technical application managers, architects, or business analysts, but sometimes also as software developers in agile software development projects directly on the business side. Accordingly, projects implemented in this way benefit from an improved business IT alignment, as a result of better demand management and requirements engineering. Due to the close integration, IT employees gain good insight into the business unit processes and, thus, understand their requirements and needs much better. In addition, they often have more credibility and trust than is the case with traditional and impersonal cooperation models. However, a later approach whereby a mixed departmental approach incorporates the co-location approach, based on the business side, is not without its challenges. If, at some point, the IT experts switch to the business side in a disciplined way, the IT department loses process know-how. It may, thus, potentially disqualify itself from digital transformation—unless it makes a clear value contribution elsewhere.

> **Overview: Shadow IT as a Lived Practice**
> - Due to relatively slow coordination and implementation processes, as well as long development cycles, the IT department is perceived as being a service provider instead of a creative innovator.

(continued)

- As a result of the increased pressure for change and ever more convenient sourcing opportunities, the business units are becoming more and more independent with regard to IT solutions.
- The result is the shadow IT phenomenon, which is usually regarded as problematic, but can also be a driver of innovation.
- In our opinion, the separation of business and IT is outdated, because IT innovations should be created where they will be used—in the business departments.
- We believe that, in future, IT innovations will be created through the close cooperation between business and IT; this will turn the "official shadow IT" into a lived practice.
- The co-location approach can serve as a transition model for the proposed organizational change.

References

1. Twentyman, J. (2016, January). *CIOs start to view 'shadow IT' as a catalyst for innovation*. Global Intelligence for the CIO. http://www.i-cio.com/innovation/consumerization/item/how-cios-start-to-view-shadow-it-as-a-catalyst-for-innovation
2. Lubich, H. (2013, Juli 8). Chancen und Risiken im Umgang mit der Schatten-IT. *swissICT Magazin*. http://www.fhnw.ch/technik/imvs/publikationen/artikel-2013/chancen-und-risiken-im-umgang-mit-der-schatten-it
3. Rentrop, C., van Laak, O., & Mevius, M. (2011). Schatten-IT: ein Thema für die Iterne Revision? *Revisionspraxis, 2*, 68–75.
4. Saat, J., & Dirding, P. (2016, January). "Legalize IT"—Sinnvoller Umgang mit Schatten-IT. *BANKING HUB*. https://bankinghub.de/banking/technology/legalize-it-sinnvoller-umgang-mit-schatten-it
5. Seidel, B. (2014, January 2). Schatten-IT ist Notwehr. *Computerwoche*. http://www.computerwoche.de/a/schatten-it-ist-notwehr,2546588
6. Moutafis, J. (2015, November 19). Eine neue Rolle für die IT. *ChannelPartner*. http://www.channelpartner.de/a/eine-neue-rolle-fuer-die-it,3218354

Innovations Through Networks: Turning Strategic Suppliers into Innovation Partners

There are two reasons why digitalization will lead to greater dependency on external partners than ever before: First, the gradual reduction of vertical IT integration leads to a shift whereby activities are externally outsourced. The keywords in this context are IT outsourcing and cloud computing. Second, the digitalization of many companies requires skills and competences that are not yet available. Although these can be developed in-house, it takes time, which is rarely available. For this reason, partnerships and networks will become more important. For example, trends such as smart grid or smart home technologies will have a lasting impact on the energy sector. Intelligent systems can search for relevant patterns based on mass data concerning the usage behavior of energy consumers to optimize energy consumption, as well as energy generation and supply. However, only a few energy companies have the necessary IT know-how to implement these disruptive innovations completely on their own. In such a case, strategic partnerships with technology companies can be an option to address the lack of competence. In the following, we describe and discuss the trend towards innovation partnerships. We first review the traditional sourcing strategies and their limitations.

Traditional IT Sourcing with a Focus on Cost Efficiency and Quality Improvement

In the past, the vertical integration of many IT departments was comparatively high. Only hardware and software, as well as selective consulting and development services, were sourced externally. This situation has already changed fundamentally in recent years. Many companies have outsourced parts of their IT value creation to external partners. These include, for example, operating IT infrastructures, the service desk, or application development. This trend is subsumed under the term IT outsourcing and has developed over the past two decades into an established procurement option for strategic IT management. The continuously rising growth

© Springer International Publishing AG, part of Springer Nature 2019
N. Urbach, F. Ahlemann, *IT Management in the Digital Age*, Management for Professionals, https://doi.org/10.1007/978-3-319-96187-3_6

rates of the outsourcing market also reflect this. For example, the Information Services Group announced that, in 2014, the global annual contract volume in the outsourcing market rose by 16% with 1218 contracts to EUR 18.5 billion (4% increase), thereby achieving the second highest result on a global scale [1].

By IT outsourcing, we mean the transfer—through contractual agreements—of all, or part of the technical and human resources, as well as the responsibility for the provision of IT services, to an external provider [2]. The benefits that companies generally intend to derive from IT outsourcing can be divided into economic, qualitative, and technological benefits. The specific strategic goals of IT management determine which of the three potential benefits are in the foreground. The economic benefit potential of IT outsourcing relates primarily to reducing the costs of services—particularly by drawing on the expertise and economies of scale of the external service provider. Furthermore, the financial flexibility of IT costs is often targeted by converting the fixed costs of internal IT to volume-dependent, variable costs on the part of the service provider. The qualitative benefits usually relate to an increase in service quality. This can be achieved primarily by having access to well-trained employees and by implementing professional processes in IT service management. The technological usage potentials aim at utilizing modern technologies without corresponding investments, which are intended to counteract technological obsolescence, due to dynamic changes in the IT environment.

These usage potentials are offset by an increase in transaction costs (primarily due to the necessary service provider management), a loss of flexibility, as well as conflicting goals of the service provider and the outsourcing organization [3]. Despite numerous cases of corporate IT (or parts of it) being outsourced successfully, the IT outsourcing topic has always been accompanied by intensive user discussions. Already in the early 1990s, successful outsourcing was recognized as a process that is not straightforward [4]. Although a large number of companies have been able to gain experience with outsourcing since then, the basic challenges have not changed until today [5]. Especially in recent times, the benefits of IT outsourcing have been increasingly questioned, often in the context of announcements by companies that they would not be extending the existing IT outsourcing contracts after their terms had expired [6].

Cloud computing (see chapter "Infrastructure as commodity: IT infrastructure services are traded on free markets and purchased as required" and "The end of the IT department: IT experts become part of the business departments and are coordinated by a dedicated executive responsibility") is a recent trend, which is also experiencing strong growth. The use of standardized external IT services associated with cloud computing can be understood as a special case of IT outsourcing, if the corresponding services have previously been provided internally. Cloud computing's special edge is that services can be accessed dynamically (elasticity—supply and demand are dynamically adapted to each other). In addition to the other benefits of outsourcing, costs can also be varied and vendor lock-ins reduced. This means that it is easier to switch providers, especially when using highly standardized, homogeneous, and simple services (such as storage). Cloud computing is therefore particularly suitable for procuring "commodity IT," which has no particular differentiating effect on the company.

The majority of the current IT departments follow a simple and convincing paradigm: Non-differentiating parts of the IT value chain can and should be provided by external service providers with more competence, lower costs, better risk control, and a more intensive focus on the actual strategic issues. Although large companies often follow this philosophy, it is not uncommon for large companies to set up their own group companies for IT, since the volume of IT services is so large that it becomes worthwhile to bundle and create their own services. Here, any economies of scale are realized by the company itself.

In principle, we believe that this trend towards shortening IT value chains will continue, with a shift in the specific outsourcing business to non-specific—highly standardized—cloud offerings. The reason for this is the increasing standardization of IT infrastructure, applications, and business processes. This standardization reduces the need for enterprise-specific customization and integration efforts, and simplifies the use of cloud solutions. However, it will not remain so. External organizations are increasingly becoming partners in strategic digitalization projects.

Joint Innovation Work with Selected Partners

The increasing innovation activity that is based on new information and communication technologies, requires new skills from traditional IT departments. In addition to the basic ability to establish efficient and effective innovation processes, new technological competencies are required, which many companies do not currently have. Technology trends, such as the using massively scalable cloud infrastructures, big data, predictive data analytics, and machine learning, require know-how that is often only available from specialized technology providers. Companies that want to develop new products and services on the basis of these technologies and conceptual approaches face the problem that the internal acquisition of corresponding knowledge and skills is risky and time-consuming. It is risky, because there are no guarantees that the necessary expertise can be achieved at all. Often, the necessary experts are not available and cannot be easily recruited for a company. It is time-consuming, because research and development activities often involve several years of work. For this reason, companies are searching for other ways to access the necessary competencies. Since the acquisition of corresponding specialized suppliers is not a suitable option in many cases, cooperation models are particularly considered. In an equal partnership, both companies can contribute their individual know-how and jointly implement innovations. Non-IT companies usually deliver market access, a deeper understanding of the customer, and product ideas. Technology companies have the skills to implement appropriate solutions. An example of this is the automobile manufacturer, Volvo, which established a partnership with Microsoft with the aim of developing new automotive technologies. They are working together on using Microsoft's augmented reality glasses—HoloLens—for their sales. They will also jointly work on the "autonomous driving" and "connected car" concepts [7]. Microsoft also established a similar cooperation with ThyssenKrupp. This involves digitalizing elevators, which, in future, will store status data directly in a cloud-based software solution to optimize maintenance activities [8].

Such partnerships can also have a network character, so that more than two companies can participate in the realization of an innovation idea. In particular, small enterprises with very specialized skills and limited investment opportunities choose such an approach, which under certain conditions can also be supported by public funds [9]. For example, work has already commenced in a corporate network to develop a system for the digital real-time monitoring of energy networks with the aim of ensuring continuous and secure provision of electricity in times of energy change [10].

The (Potentially) Difficult Relationship with Innovation Partners

Relationships between innovation partners are usually complex and occur at different levels. Mutual trust is necessary, because it is usually a matter of long-term cooperation, which can imply disclosing existing or developing new intellectual property (IP). After all, there is a risk that one side will behave opportunistically and use the gained knowledge to the detriment of the other side. In addition, such partnerships are associated with a great deal of uncertainty and comprehensive contracts are usually not feasible.

It is particularly difficult if there are several relationship levels between the partners. For example, a situation may arise in which a technology partner provides important know-how for digital innovations on the one hand, but is also a "normal" supplier of products (hardware and software) and services on the other. Therefore, the question arises whether the industrial partner is free to purchase products and services from other suppliers. Conversely, the technology company can also be a customer of the industrial partner. Coopetition relationships, in which there is "cooperation" in one market segment and "competition" between the partners in another market segment, are also critical.

The complexity of partner relationships means that partnerships need to be carefully planned, nurtured and, above all, systematically managed, more than ever before.

Innovation Partnerships Are Not a Purchasing Task

Innovation partnerships cannot be established by purchasing departments that traditionally try to optimize procurement conditions in terms of costs, quality, and time. Instead, it requires understanding each other's side well, building lasting trust, dismantling points of conflict, as well as developing a vision and sharing strategic goals. Current IT and purchasing functions are often not yet designed for this. Although advanced organizations already have a supplier portfolio management system in place, but this also focuses less on strategic partnerships than on bundling needs and optimizing procurement conditions.

However, in times of digitalization, IT innovation partnerships require a new approach that goes far beyond purchasing processes, and is closely linked to demand, as well as innovation management processes. Based on early innovation ideas that have already been developed, it is necessary to systematically search for suitable partners whose suitability is then thoroughly tested. The following criteria, for example, can be used here: Whether a potential partner has experience of the other potential partner's industry, compatibility of incentive and governance systems, the strategic importance of cooperation for the potential partner, and matching technological competence. Finally, the participants will be invited to address and examine their basic willingness to cooperate. If this is the case, a common vision and cooperation model can be developed, thereby resulting in contractual agreements. Then, they can begin to jointly realize new products and services. This opening to the outside world necessitates a cultural change, which takes time. In many companies, discussing long-term corporate goals with (potential) partners and realizing them together, is not yet conceivable. After all, the partner may gain deep insights into business processes and the company's innovation activities.

On the Way to Innovation Partnerships

Sustainable management of innovation partnerships requires new and changed processes and structures, new roles and responsibilities, as well as cultural change. In order to realize innovations by using external partners, particularly following factors have to be considered:

The management of innovation partners is not an isolated process, but can be integrated with *IT innovation management* or *IT demand management*. As soon as innovative ideas and concepts or far-reaching requirements from the business units become available, it is necessary to check whether the own capabilities and resources are sufficient for the realization or whether external partners are required. If the latter is the case, partner management becomes active.

Innovation partnerships will only be successful if the partner fits the company and its goals. It is therefore important to systematically monitor the market environment to identify suitable partners. *Partner* and *technology scouting* cannot be carried out separately, because it goes without saying that it is also necessary to check which specific technological competencies are required and which potential partners possess these skills. Partner scouting can be a continuous process—especially if a company's level of innovation is very high and there is a constant need for establishing new partnerships. In such cases, the company usually searches simultaneously for possible candidates with a view to acquire them. In many cases, however, it is only actioned when there is a concrete need.

Partner portfolio management is particularly useful for organizations that maintain a large number of innovation partnerships. This approach aims at enabling a systematic and comprehensive management of partnerships. Partner portfolio management tasks include defining criteria for selecting partners, establishing corporate transparency regarding partnerships, ensuring consistent partner communication, and monitoring the quality of collaboration.

An essential element of initiating innovation partnerships is the development of mutually acceptable contracts. In order to keep the corresponding development efforts as low as possible, companies with many innovation partnerships find it particularly useful to develop *contractual frameworks*, which are then adapted to the respective partnerships. These frameworks should include all critical elements of cooperation, such as joint intellectual property, exploitation rights, or profit sharing.

Scientific studies have shown time and again that positive personal relationships between the actors involved are a key success factor for strategic corporate cooperation [11, 12]. Unsurprisingly, there is a regular need for *relationship management*. This should help to foster regular personal contacts at all involved levels.

Relationship management is closely linked to the need for reaching consensus on *common strategic goals*. This requires adequate and thorough communication between the actors involved. In addition, the targets should be documented. They can and should be part of the agreement.

Due to the frequently complex relationship with innovation partners, it is important that consistent communication takes place. In this way, different organizational units approaching an innovation partner in an uncoordinated way with different concerns, can be avoided. This requires clear governance that regulates who is responsible for which type of communication with the innovation partners. At the same time, there should also be transparency within the organization regarding the cooperation with the innovation partner. As outlined above, governance is closely linked to portfolio management.

Establishing the management of innovation partners as described here, is not an easy process. As with all far-reaching organizational changes, change management requires convincing employees of transformation's usefulness and motivating them to go along with the implementation in a constructive and committed manner. Communication, participation, and training are effective instruments here.

Institutionalization of Partner Management

In companies, the management of innovation partners can be performed by different organizational units. In principle, IT innovation management or the business development function can be considered: Establishing a presence in *IT innovation management* makes sense, because there is a special understanding of the partner's specific skills and resources. The disadvantage is that the necessary processes and structures have to be newly created. If partner management is seen from the long-term perspective of business development, this responsibility can also be given to the *business development function*. There is, however, usually only a limited understanding of the skills and resources mentioned above.

Overview: Innovations Through Networks
- A purely service- and efficiency-oriented IT department is not sufficient to meet the digitalization requirements.
- The trend towards outsourcing will continue, with cloud-based approaches gaining in importance.
- In addition, new innovation partnerships with selected technology companies will be established.
- These innovation partnerships help fill any competency and resource gaps.
- However, such partnerships can be difficult due to the multi-tiered nature of the relationship.
- For this reason, centrally coordinated partner management is necessary to ensure the targeted selection, initiation, establishment, and management of partnerships.
- Such partner management can be institutionalized in various ways.

References

1. Information Services Group. (2014, February 2). Starkes Jahr in EMEA—Mega Deals um 25% gestiegen. http://www.isg-one.com/DE/news/150202-DE.asp
2. Clark, T. D., Jr., Zmud, R. W., & McCray, G. E. (1995). The outsourcing of information services: Transforming the nature of business in the information industry. *Journal of Information Technology, 10*(4), 221–237.
3. Grover, V., Cheon, M. J., & Teng, J. T. C. (1996). The effect of service quality and partnership on the outsourcing of information systems functions. *Journal of Management Information Systems, 12*(4), 89–116.
4. Lacity, M. C., & Hirschheim, R. (1993). The information systems outsourcing bandwagon. *Sloan Management Review, 35*(1), 73–86.
5. Buchwald, A., Urbach, N., & Würz, T. (2014). IT-Outsourcing ist kein Selbstläufer. *Wirtschaftsinformatik and Management, 2014*(3), 30–38.
6. Tödtmann, C. (2013, March 27). Vorwärts im Rückwärtsgang—Insourcen ist profitabler als Outsourcen. *WirtschaftsWoche.* http://blog.wiwo.de/management/2013/03/27/vorwarts-im-ruckwartsgang-insourcen-ist-profitabler-als-outsourcen-meint-it-organisationsprofi-robin-protzmann/
7. Nagel, P. (2015, November 20). Entwicklung neuer Automobiltechniken: Volvo kooperiert mit Microsoft. *automotiveIT.* http://www.automotiveit.eu/volvo-kooperiert-mit-microsoft/news/id-0051314
8. Dörner, A. (2015, October 27). Neue Kooperation: Der Aufzug geht in die Cloud. *Handelsblatt.* http://www.handelsblatt.com/technik/it-internet/neue-kooperation-der-aufzug-geht-in-die-cloud/12506704.html
9. Bundesministerium für Wirtschaft und Energie. (2016a). *Zentrales Innovationsprogramm Mittelstand (ZIM).* Kooperationsnetzwerke und ihre FuE-Projekte. http://www.zim-bmwi.de/kooperationsnetzwerke
10. Bundesministerium für Wirtschaft und Energie. (2016b). *Zentrales Innovationsprogramm Mittelstand (ZIM).* Neueste Beispiele geförderter FuE-Projekte. http://www.zim-bmwi.de/erfolgsbeispiele

11. Lee, J.-N., & Kim, Y.-G. (1999). Effect of partnership quality on IS outsourcing success: Conceptual framework and empirical validation. *Journal of Management Information Systems, 15*(4), 29–61.
12. Mohr, J., & Spekman, R. (1994). Characteristics of partnership success: Partnership attributes, communication behavior, and conflict resolution techniques. *Strategic Management Journal, 15*(2), 135–152.

Focusing on the User: Development Processes are Agile, End-User-Centered, and Merged with the Operation

In many companies, software development processes are largely organized according to the waterfall model. Therefore, the different development phases occur sequentially from analyzing the requirements to the specialized and technical conception, implementation and testing and all the way to the go-live—usually with minimal feedback possibilities between the phases. Development activities focus strongly on technology and function, while user needs and acceptance have hardly been taken into account thus far. This approach appears to be limited in its suitability for the demands of the digital world. If the traditional software development processes from the corporate context were applied to the development of modern apps in the consumer context, there would only be an update every few months or even years. The app would therefore not be successful on the market, since users are presently accustomed to continuous background updates—and therefore to always having up-to-date applications. In times of digitalization, more and more application systems are also aimed at company external users, such as apps for customer service, marketing or sales, but also portals for suppliers and partners, so that user interface design, in particular, becomes a competitive differentiating activity. At the same time, the employees themselves are also becoming increasingly demanding. Particularly the digital natives—people who grew up in the digital world—are becoming less and less tolerant towards poor user-friendliness of software systems.

We therefore believe that an alignment of software development processes will be necessary. Development processes that are known from the development of consumer-oriented software products will serve as models here. We foresee a far greater spread of agile approaches in future, especially for the development of "lightweight IT," which we understand as front-end dominated and end-customer oriented systems [1]. The main idea of the agile approaches is that a first deployment of rudimentary solutions takes place at a very early stage and these are then further developed iteratively with the help of user feedback. In general, the user features more prominently in the foreground of development activities. Last but not least, software development and operation will continue to merge.

© Springer International Publishing AG, part of Springer Nature 2019
N. Urbach, F. Ahlemann, *IT Management in the Digital Age*, Management for Professionals, https://doi.org/10.1007/978-3-319-96187-3_7

Traditional Software Development Processes Usually Follow the Waterfall Model

The majority of companies use the waterfall model to develop new software. It is one of the older and best-known software engineering models, which Winston Royce, the American computer science researcher, mentioned as far back as 1970 [2]. This is a linear—not iterative—phase model in which the results of a phase enter the following phase—like a waterfall—as binding specifications. The typical phases of the waterfall model are the requirements analysis, professional and technical conception, implementation, software testing, as well as delivery, deployment, and maintenance. Each phase has predefined start and end points with clearly defined results. However, variants of the simple waterfall model have been developed, which allow reverse jumps to previous phases if something goes wrong in a current phase. The possibilities of turning back between phases are generally very limited.

There are good reasons for the dominance of the waterfall model. The different phases are clearly distinguishable from each other and this enables a division of work in projects, which is essential for very large development projects. Projects organized according to the waterfall model are, thus, comparatively easy to manage, since planning and progress control of the phases is usually quite simple; traditional project management is based on this paradigm. Due to its simplicity, the model is also very easy to communicate and easy to understand—even for inexperienced employees. But most of all, it is a very efficient procedure model if the requirements for the software to be developed and the available budget framework remain stable for the duration of the project.

In addition to the strong influence that the sequential flow of the development process has, the development activities in many companies are characterized by their strong technological and functional orientation. The main success criteria are, above all, that the developed application systems cover—in the best possible way—the technical requirements placed on them and that they meet the typical non-functional requirements, such as reliability, performance, and efficiency. User needs and acceptance, on the other hand, are often only taken into account to a limited extent during application development. Software is usually developed for a very specific type of device and has a less modern user interface design. User interface experts (UI experts) are only very rarely involved in the development process. More often than not, the programmers, who are mainly responsible for the implementation of the functionality, do the UI development on the side.

The Future of Software Development Is Agile

Under the general conditions of the "non-digital" world, the established software development approaches can be regarded as quite suitable. Especially in the case of stable requirements, new application systems can be developed efficiently—particularly for very large projects. However, they often lead to demarcation problems between the different phases and are characterized by a lack of flexibility to deal with late changes in the development process. A major disadvantage is the very long period of time that it takes from the requirements analysis to the introduction of the developed system. The functional requirements are often outdated when the user comes into contact with a new application for the first time, or he has problems to articulate the requirements in a suitable way. It is thus not surprising that the final product does not always meet the expectations of the customer. However, rapid implementation of technological innovations is crucial in the digitalized business world—a short "time-to-market" is increasingly becoming a business-critical success factor. Furthermore, user satisfaction is becoming an important criterion. Corporate IT is therefore required to meet the requirements of this new world. New approaches are needed that enable significantly faster innovation and implementation cycles, and that are geared for user expectations. If the IT department continues with its old behavioral patterns, there is a serious risk that the business units will simply become active without involving corporate IT, because of the increased pressure to change (see chapter "Shadow IT as a lived practice: IT innovations are developed in interdisciplinary teams within the business departments"). As a result, the "shadow IT" is created, which leads to compliance and security risks, as well as corporate IT increasingly losing its right of existence.

For the above-mentioned reasons, we predict far more agile approaches to software development projects in the future IT department than at present. The core idea of agile software development is its iterative, incremental approach. Instead of a complete ex-ante specification of the product to be developed, the work starts with a product vision, which—in principle –still leaves room for deviations. The development project is divided into several time stages within the project planning context, at the end of which there is a product increment, namely a fully functional intermediate product. These product increments are presented to the client to give feedback for the following development phase. A similar procedure is very often observed in the consumer sector (app principle). The providers of modern apps often launch relatively simple versions of their applications on the market at a very early stage. Continuous updates are then used so that the functionality is gradually extended and adapted to the users' needs.

The idea of agile software development is not new—the first approaches were already discussed in the early 1990s. The agile approach received a significant boost when the American software developer, Kent Beck, published the first book on "Extreme Programming" in 1999 [3]. With his approach, Beck presented a method that places a programming task's solution in the foreground of software development whilst simultaneously attaching less importance to a formalized procedure—which is the core of the agile software development idea. The term "agile" was established a little later in 2001 by the "agile manifesto," which was formulated at a meeting of 17 renowned software developers and subsequently published. At the heart of this manifesto, are four guiding principles: (1) Individuals and interactions are more important than processes and tools, (2) functioning software takes precedence over comprehensive documentation, (3) working with customers is more important than contract negotiations, and (4) responding to change is more important than following a plan. The signatories of the manifesto also suggest principles for operationalizing these four central values. They include early and continuous software delivery, close cooperation between business units and software developers, motivational measures, attention to technical excellence, and self-organizing teams [4]. Since then, agile approaches in different forms have become increasingly popular. In addition to the already mentioned extreme programming, Scrum [5] and Kanban [6] are among the most established and best-known approaches. There are also growing discussions and attempts to use agile approaches outside software development, for example in product or organizational development.

At this stage, we draw attention to the fact that, in future, there will still be areas in which an agile approach is not appropriate and in which a linear approach (i.e., following the waterfall model) would be preferable. A major argument on this point is that agile approaches are usually not freely scalable and therefore tend to suit smaller, narrowly defined projects better. Furthermore, there will also be future projects with contextual conditions in which the traditional, non-agile approaches can fully exploit their strengths. From our point of view, the agile approaches will be particularly suitable for "lightweight IT" where they will demonstrate their strengths. This includes particularly those application systems that are primarily geared for the end customer and/or consumer, or that are aimed at employees—for example in sales—who are in direct contact with this target group. These are mostly front-end dominated applications that are optimized for use on mobile devices, such as smartphones or tablets. As a rule, these "light systems" are not considered critical infrastructures of a company and are therefore not considered essential for its business activities; instead, it is understood as innovative "gadgets," which form the basis for new business models. In contrast, for the "heavyweight IT" the traditional procedure models of software development are preferred. These are mainly back-end dominated systems, which are typically highly complex and can be regarded as critical infrastructure for the respective companies. In contrast to "lightweight IT," stability and security are much more important here than innovation and user-friendliness [1].

Stronger Focus on the End User

The close involvement of the user in the development process is an inherent characteristic of agile procedure models (see above). However, developing innovative and intuitive user interfaces also requires new skills within the IT departments of many companies. Recent studies showed that the acceptance and success of information systems are significantly influenced by the so-called "hedonic value," which is the added fun during use [7]. Young users, in particular, are less and less willing to accept outdated operating concepts, because through their private use of modern tablets and smartphones, they are accustomed to high-quality user interfaces. The development of good operating concepts becomes thus a success factor for the provision of new technological solutions. Since only a few companies currently have sufficient competence in this area, the majority of companies first have to establish it or source it externally (see chapter "Innovations through networks: turning strategic suppliers into innovation partners").

The increasing user focus requires new software development and deployment paradigms. Instead of a purely technical monitoring of hardware and software, comprehensive user monitoring enables a better understanding of user behavior and, finally, the development of user-specific applications. While planning committees previously made decisions based on design changes, in future their decisions will be based on user feedback. Experiments with design variants can be executed during use to achieve—step-by-step—an optimal design. Such A/B tests have already been used for several years in e-commerce to improve the conversion rate of online shops. Instead of extensive testing prior to software deployment, the future approach will also include testing while the new applications are already in use. This approach enables faster deployment of new releases and a dynamic response to problems, as well as deficits, regardless of strict release times. Accordingly, the innovation and release cycles are reduced from several months to a few days, exactly as the user knows it from the private context in which smartphone apps are usually updated in the background on a regular basis without the users even knowing about it.

The concept of "gamification" represents a recent trend towards enhancing—with a user focus—the attractiveness of software applications. This refers to the use of typical elements, such as high scores, experience points, or awards, in a non-gaming context [8]. The main goal of gamification is to increase the motivation for performing otherwise monotonous and less demanding, or unpopular, activities via playful elements. Thereby, it becomes possible to address those generations for whom playing with game consoles was an important element of their youth. One example of how gamification can be used in the corporate context is Danone's in-house innovation promotion platform. Depending on their individual contribution to this platform, employees can attain bronze, silver, or gold status. In this way, the platform aims at motivating employees to participate in the innovation process and helping select, as well as implement, ideas [9]. Another example is Bayer AG's online simulation game, "International Management Simulation." Here, the user aims at acquiring new business management knowledge in a playful way by passing through management processes in fast motion. Several teams compete as companies with each other in simulated fiscal years by introducing certain products in different markets, thereby asserting themselves against the other teams [10]. We believe, however, that before gamification is put to productive use across the board, the concept must first prove itself in day-to-day business. Nevertheless, we presume that it will be increasingly taken into account when designing and developing application systems in the years ahead. It remains to be seen whether this is a passing fashion or a sustainable trend.

Merger of Development and Operation

Corporate IT's key challenge in the age of digitalization is to respond quickly to new customer requirements and innovations while ensuring high-performance and stable IT operations. The response times to internal and external customers' change requests, as well as the time-to-market of new business models, will be decisive for the economic success of the entire company. As already discussed, agile development processes can significantly increase application update rates. However, these measures only reach their full impact if the applications are put, just as dynamically, into the production operation. When traditional quality and operational processes are used, it is not uncommon for several days, or even weeks, to pass before new or updated application systems are put into the production operation. In order to respond flexibly and quickly to new business requirements, development and operation must work together more closely and coordinate their processes better. The keyword, DevOps, which is much discussed in recent months, represents a solution to this challenge [11]. This involves the merger of *development* and *operations*. The core idea of the approach is to transfer agile methods to IT operations and to combine the procedure models, which are used for software development, with IT operations. This minimizes the risk of untested elements in production, since the same processes are used identically and without interruptions throughout the entire software life cycle.

Although it appears that no precise definition of DevOps has emerged thus far—at least not in academic research—the five basic principles proposed by Jez Humble, one of the pioneers of the DevOps movement, have been widely disseminated and accepted [12]. Accordingly, the framework of DevOps is formed by culture, automation, lean, measurement, and sharing (CALMS). The *cultural* basis of DevOps is the trustful cooperation between developers, testers, and administrators, a constant flow of information, and a continuous willingness to learn. *Automation* of work processes is an important prerequisite for the successful implementation of DevOps. The spectrum covers the mapping of simple recurring activities and the full automation of the development and operations of entire environments. A *lean* implementation relies on avoiding waste, creating transparency, and optimizing the process holistically. In order to ensure the quality of implementation throughout, uniform *measurement* criteria must be defined. Here, traceable metrics should enable continuous improvement measures, as well as monitoring the entire application, its components, and the underlying processes. Last but not least, the willingness to share knowledge, learning from each other, and *sharing* knowledge proactively, are all part of an effective and efficient DevOps implementation. As is the case with the agile approach to application development, it is also important to emphasize that the DevOps concept is less associated with implementing and further developing core functionalities of critical systems as is the case with the "light systems," such as graphical user interfaces, reporting applications, or even simple workflow applications.

Two-Speed IT as a Harbinger of Agile IT

In order to meet the demands of the digital world, we increasingly expect the use of agile, end-user-centered, software development processes that have merged with operations. As we have already mentioned on several occasions, this specifically does not mean that the company's entire application landscape will change to this new world of thought from one day to the next. Instead, it is important to determine for which areas "fast" IT can be advantageous and where traditional approaches are still justified. Accordingly, our recommendations to the IT management in this regard are to successively build up the necessary competencies and to pilot selected applications for (further) development. For many companies, the development of the necessary structures, processes, methods, and tools should not be a major challenge. Instead, we expect that a cultural change, as well as the development of willingness, commitment, and skills on the part of the employees will be a far greater challenge. However, as soon as these competencies have been developed and tested in several application cases, the medium-term task is to classify the application portfolio according to the distinction between "heavyweight" and "lightweight." This distinction must then also be taken into account in architecture management, because it requires more flexible architectures (see chapter "Transformable IT landscapes: IT architectures are standardized, modular, flexible, ubiquitous, elastic, cost-effective, and secure"). Furthermore, we recommend a systematic separation of back-end and front-end development, since front-end development has a stronger association with the "light" world, whereas the predominantly monolithic back-end systems are presumably already in good hands in the traditional world.

Due to the suggested division of application development into an agile, "light," and dynamic world on the one hand, and a linear, "heavy," and security-oriented world on the other, the question that arises is what implications these developments have for the organizational structure of corporate IT. In the past few months, the concept of bimodal IT or "two-speed IT" was discussed very intensively in this context. The term bimodal IT was coined by Gartner Analysts and describes the division of the IT department into the management of secure and predictable core systems (Mode 1), and quite experimental, agile, and customer-oriented applications (Mode 2) [13]. The basic idea is to create a type of fast track for high-priority, high-speed digital transformation projects in addition to the traditional IT development and IT operations structure. The first step is to develop the core systems further, based on clearly defined requirements, as well as the "stability and reliability" paradigm. The second step focuses on "disruptive" IT solutions and is accordingly characterized by customer- or business-driven digital transformation projects. Here, the main focus is on "innovation and differentiation [14]." Following our argumentation stated in chapter "Development and operation are not decisive: IT management follows the "innovate-design-transform" paradigm", the IT department in Mode 1 will continue working according to the traditional *plan-build-run* paradigm, while, in Mode 2, it will be working according to the *innovate-design-transform* paradigm that we suggest. In our opinion, the follow-up question that arises is whether "two-speed IT" is a sustainable organizational solution for establishing corporate IT. Assuming that no business sector will be spared digitalization (see chapter "No business without IT: IT is the central and indispensable driver of entrepreneurial value creation"), we regard bimodal IT merely as a transitional solution for the first years of the digital transformation. In future, we expect business and IT areas to interlink much closer (see chapter "Shadow IT as a lived practice: IT innovations are developed in interdisciplinary teams within the business departments"), we expect a much more far-reaching shift of IT operations to the cloud (see chapter "Infrastructure as commodity: IT infrastructure services are traded on free markets and purchased as required"), and finally, we expect the end of the IT department as it is currently structured (see chapter "The end of the IT department: IT experts become part of the business departments and are coordinated by a dedicated executive responsibility").

Overview: Focusing on the User

- In the digital era, the speed with which new software is made available and updated (time-to-market), is becoming increasingly important.
- The design and usability of applications are becoming more important, due to a stronger customer and partner focus, as well as more demanding user groups.
- The traditional software development processes, which are often organized according to the waterfall model, only have a limited suitability in meeting the new requirements.
- In future, we expect a significant increase in the dissemination of agile approaches, especially for the development of front-end and end-user-oriented applications.
- The end user is increasingly in the foreground of software development activities, and this requires new software development and deployment paradigms.
- With DevOps, agile methods are transferred to IT operations, and the process models used for software development are merged with the process models used for IT operations.
- The idea behind bimodal IT is to create an "organizational fast lane" for digital transformation projects, in addition to the traditional IT development and IT operations structure.

References

1. Bygstad, B. (2015, May 26–29). The coming of lightweight IT. In *Proceedings of the 23rd European Conference on Information Systems (ECIS 2015)*. Münster.
2. Royce, W. W. (1970, August). Managing the development of large software system. In *Proceedings of IEEE WESCON*.
3. Beck, K. (1999). *Extreme programming explained: Embrace change*. Boston: Addison-Wesley Professional.

4. Beck, K, Beedle, M., Bennekum, A., Cockburn, A., Cunningham, W., Fowler, M. et al. (2001). *Manifesto for agile software development*. http://www.agilemanifesto.org/
5. Beedle, M., & Schwaber, K. (2002). *Agile software development with scrum*. Upper Saddle River, NJ: Prentice Hall.
6. Anderson, D. J. (2010). *Kanban: Successful evolutionary change for your technology business*. Sequim, WA: Blue Hole Press.
7. Whitten, D., Hightower, R., & Sayeed, L. (2014, Fall). Mobile device adaptation efforts: The impact of hedonic and utilitarian value, *J Computer Information Systems, 55*, 48–58.
8. Deterding, S., Khaled, R., Nacke, L. E., & Dixon D. (2011, May 7–12). Gamification: Toward a definition. In *Proceedings of the CHI 2011 2011*. Vancouver, BC. http://hci.usask.ca/uploads/219-02-Deterding,-Khaled,-Nacke,-Dixon.pdf
9. Quack, K. (2013, April 15). Eine soziale Plattform fördert Ideen zur Reife. *Computerwoche*. http://www.computerwoche.de/a/eine-soziale-plattform-foerdert-ideen-zur-reife,2536036
10. Bayer, A. G. (2016). *Bayer international management simulation*. http://www.bimsonline.com/
11. Hüttermann, M. (2012). *DevOps for developers. Integrate development and operations. The agile way*. New York: Apress.
12. Appdynamcis. (2015). Keep CALM and embrace Devops. *White Paper*. https://www.appdynamics.com/lp/keep-calm-and-embrace-devops/
13. Gartner. (2016). *Bimodal IT, IT Glossary*. http://www.gartner.com/it-glossary/bimodal
14. Laitenberger, O. (2015, December 22). Digitale Disruption trifft auch die IT-Abteilungen. *Computerwoche*. http://www.computerwoche.de/a/digitale-disruption-trifft-auch-die-it-abteilungen,3220993

Infrastructure as Commodity: IT Infrastructure Services Are Traded on Free Markets and Purchased as Required

In the context of the developments described above, IT infrastructures will be more important than ever before. In future, not only individual business processes, but also entire business models and the continued existence of companies, will depend on the stability, availability, adaptability, and security of IT infrastructures. Furthermore, infrastructure services are presently more standardized, which is why the term "commodity IT" has become established. Specialized service providers can offer a quality that many companies do not achieve in their own IT departments. The question why an internal IT department should still operate its own IT infrastructures, arises in this context. In fact, we predict that the future corporate IT will only in isolated cases use their own servers, configure middleware, and install security patches, and we assume that external service providers will completely take over these parts of the IT value chain. That is not all: Virtualization technologies, cloud solutions, as well as the increasing standardization and precise specification of infrastructure service types and performance classes will create entirely new markets. IT infrastructure services are traded on markets and can be purchased as easily as drawing electricity from the wall socket.

IT Infrastructures Versus Business Applications

However, the scenario of highly standardized IT services, which are freely traded on stock exchanges and other markets, is only expected for technologies that are used in practically all companies and that have no differentiation potential. These include, for example, networks, storage services, computing capacity, database services, virtual computers, basic big data services, or directory services. In addition, there are application systems that, to a large extent, do not depend on specific business processes and models, and that can often be used "as-is," namely without special configuration or system integration requirements. These include e-mail systems, unified messaging solutions, as well as groupware and collaboration platforms.

© Springer International Publishing AG, part of Springer Nature 2019
N. Urbach, F. Ahlemann, *IT Management in the Digital Age*, Management for Professionals, https://doi.org/10.1007/978-3-319-96187-3_8

However, we do not expect complex business application systems to be subject to these new sales and market structures. There are various reasons for this: On the one hand, there are much higher lock-in effects, that is, switching providers often makes no sense, due to the high configuration and system integration effort. In addition, there are often individual programming tasks that are difficult or even impossible to transfer to other solution providers. On the other hand, we are already experiencing increasingly standardized business processes; this will, however, not manifest itself in easily replaceable application software in the foreseeable future. We can, instead, assume that business process outsourcing will continue to prevail in areas with corresponding standardization. In addition, many companies use specific business processes to establish their competitive advantages; that is, they differentiate themselves from the competition by means of efficient, flexible, or particularly customer-oriented business processes. Extensive standardization, such as would be necessary for easily interchangeable business application systems, would nullify these benefits.

It is interesting to observe that companies presently often still diagnose the differentiation potential of their IT infrastructure or business applications, although it hardly exists anymore. For political and historical reasons, companies still use individual solutions and systems, which can easily be replaced by highly standardized architectures. However, scientific theory teaches that companies in times of increasing competitive intensity and increasing cost pressure quickly reduce such inefficiencies (or they become less competitive).

Classical IT Operation in the Internal Data Processing Center

Presently, many IT departments still operate their own data processing center or even several data processing centers. The latter applies particularly to large, multinational companies that cannot—or do not want to—go without redundancy to increase the global availability of their IT services. However, the depth of IT value creation is often already optimized, which means that external service providers are used, for example, to provide and maintain end devices, to operate the data processing center, or to take over service processes, such as the help desk. Cloud solutions are already used intensively at present, but predominantly as a "private cloud"—that is, within their own network and based on their own hardware. Nevertheless, an estimated thirty percent of infrastructure costs are already being spent on cloud solutions [1]. Business applications that are operated by external providers are purchased far less frequently. There is too much concern about privacy and security, as well as availability. In certain cases, legal requirements and regulations also make the use of such services more difficult. This classic IT operation is based on the following historical assumptions that are not sufficiently questioned by many managers: (1) Wide area networks (WANs) are either unavailable, or too expensive and inefficient, thereby making it impossible or uneconomical to purchase services remotely. (2) IT is highly company-specific and therefore requires its own IT value chain. (3) Data protection, data security, and IT stability requirements need separate operations. (4) Internal service provision is cheaper, because only the costs of IT service provision have to be covered.

Nicholas Carr [2] and others have pictorially compared this line of argumentation with the common nineteenth century practice of constructing not only industrial factories, but also a power plant that supplies the necessary energy for the production processes. At that time, nobody could have imagined that it would be possible to transport large quantities of energy of specified quality (e.g., without voltage fluctuations) over long distances and offer it at an acceptable price. It was also inconceivable to place the success-critical supply of energy in the hands of external organizations—the consequences would have been too devastating in the event of non-delivery or poor delivery. The history of industrialization and particularly the developments of the last 25 years have taught us better: Energy is reliably available all over the world in almost the same quality. Legislators have defined standards and procedures for generating, transmitting, trading, and distributing energy. On this basis, energy can now be traded on stock exchanges—independent of any transport infrastructure and specific generation processes.

We experience similar scenarios in the world of information and communication technology. In the medium term, we will face a scenario similar to the energy example. Just as the assumptions that led to the local construction of power plants no longer apply today, in a few years' time (if not already today) the assumptions underlying local IT services will no longer apply: (1) WANs are already available practically everywhere and are comparatively inexpensive and powerful. Even private WANs are affordable at present. In addition, the Internet is increasingly being used successfully to provide corporate IT services. Encryption and authentication technologies make this possible. (2) In addition, IT is, to a large extent, not company-specific. Only a few application systems can be regarded as constituting a competitive advantage and therefore require individual solutions. Presently, infrastructures can be largely standardized, and non-differentiating applications are (already nowadays) largely standardized. (3) Data protection, as well as data security and stability, do not necessarily require separate operations. Even though an own IT operation gives managers the comfort of having everything under control, this does not mean that the concerns of data protection—data security and stability—are sufficiently taken into account. On the one hand, external threats have increased. On the other hand, many managers realize that it is becoming increasingly difficult for them to ensure adequate IT security. For example, behind closed doors one hears of manipulation attempts that have been tried and often succeeded, but which rarely become public knowledge. Even without having reliable figures at our disposal, we maintain that today practically every major company has already experienced successful attacks on its own IT. Large IT service providers also have more experience, more specialists, and sufficient size to implement the necessary security measures cost-effectively for themselves and their customers. (4) Internal service provision is, in many cases, not more favorable than external service provision. Today's IT departments are often organized as cost centers, which "only" have to work in a cost-covering way. However, external service providers that aim to make a profit, are in many cases more cost-efficient, because they can achieve significant economies of scale. An external service provision is advisable particularly for small to medium-sized organizations, since establishing appropriate organizational units and providing competent staff is often too expensive (if at all possible). Nor can the same prices be achieved for hardware and software procurement, as is the case with large IT service providers. Even large companies will increasingly need to ask themselves whether operating their own IT landscapes is one of their core competencies or whether they tend to distract attention from central management issues.

Standardization as an Essential Prerequisite for Future Developments

The trends described above enable companies to outsource generic infrastructure and business application services in unprecedented ways. Extensive standardization is a prerequisite for and logical consequence of this development. The increase in standardization results from various individual trends. On the one hand, competitive pressure has increased in many segments of the IT market, which has led to crowding-out and market-consolidation developments. The markets for microprocessors, operating systems, and databases, for example, underwent a significant reduction in the number of providers in recent decades. This trend will also continue in younger or new market segments, such as the still young market for big data solutions. On the other hand, professional and trade associations, industry consortia and networks, as well as standardization institutions are working on the unification of interface technologies, file formats, and network protocols. There has been a revolution in thinking. Ten to fifteen years ago, standardization usually only began when it was unavoidable, due to technological diversity and incompatibilities, and due to customers vehemently demanding it; today's manufacturers, however, usually start working on uniform systems, processes, and protocols at a very early stage—well aware that they would otherwise have no chance of placing their products. The example of cloud services for the operation of virtual machines illustrates this development. Practically all providers have supported existing industry standards from the outset, instead of trying to define their own standards.

Since digital transformation does not only extend to individual companies, but also to cross-company value creation processes (supply chains), as well as socio-political and social spheres of life, secure and stable IT infrastructures are of particular importance for nation states and their governments. We already noticed that legislators are taking measures to safeguard critical infrastructures. In future, this will become even more pronounced with regard to IT. We can expect that there will be laws and regulations that define and enforce certain safety and stability requirements. We can therefore assume that legislators will also push ahead with the standardization of IT. They are already doing so, but predominantly only in the form of recommendations. An example is the German Federal Office for Information Security (FSI), which presented a set of rules whereby information and communication technology will be protected with IT baseline protection [3].

It is not surprising that especially those companies that offer generic IT services, rely on standards. Customers can only use their services easily and integrate them into existing IT environments quickly, if they use or build on common standards. This includes, for example, database interfaces or network protocols for accessing storage services. However, this does not yet mean that externally operated cloud infrastructures purchased from one provider would be easily transferable to another provider. This technical possibility is still in its infancy.

We can therefore assume that basic IT services will be highly standardized in future, more than ever before. This standardization promotes the comparability of offers and makes it easier to change suppliers. From the current IT department's point of view, however, the biggest advantage is that it is becoming increasingly easier to replace in-house infrastructures with cloud-based infrastructures.

IT as a Service and Commodity

The standardization of IT infrastructures has also another effect: IT services become tradable. In times of low (seasonal) demand, cloud service providers can reduce their prices and if demand is high, they can adjust prices upwards. Short-term price adjustments are possible and necessary, because customers often want to benefit from the so-called elasticity of cloud infrastructures—they only want to pay for exactly those services and capacities that they actually use. In times of low information processing (e.g., during the summer holidays), IT costs are lower; in the "hot phases" during the winter months, they are correspondingly higher. As a result, cloud service providers will be able to offer lower prices in the summer months, thereby hoping that other customers will take advantage of the freed-up capacity. On a global level, this principle makes much sense, because market mechanisms can help distribute the scarce commodity of IT as best as possible among the customers.

The next development stage will be to freely trade infrastructure services on stock exchanges. This is particularly true for very homogeneous and highly standardized IT services, because there is little uncertainty or information asymmetry for the market participants. In principle, three basic services in different forms and quality classes are possible: (1) *Processing power*: Here, cloud processing capacities—basically unused microprocessor time in mostly virtualized computer systems—are traded. (2) *Storage services*: This concerns the permanent storage of data. Presently, there are already different performance classes with different focal points in terms of storage duration, frequency of read and write accesses, and so on. (3) *Transmission power*: This concerns network bandwidth. "Priority quotas" are also conceivable, namely the assurance that your own data will be transferred, as a matter of priority, in existing network infrastructures.

We can assume that there will be operating system services or middleware—in the medium to long term—that can integrate dynamically deployed cloud resources into the user's own infrastructure in a completely transparent manner. Also, it may not matter which service provider is physically storing certain data. The only important aspects are that the availability and security requirements are met and that the service provider receives his contractually guaranteed payment for this.

Although the technical feasibility of such flexible and elastic infrastructures being traded on markets is not yet fully realized, the players involved are already preparing for this scenario. The German stock exchange has already taken the first steps towards an open market for cloud services [4]. Although this service was discontinued, due to a lack of demand [5], experts agree that an increased demand is to be expected and that the successful establishment of a corresponding stock exchange will be possible and probable in future.

Change in the Provider Spectrum

The development towards the simple purchase of highly standardized infrastructure services on free markets will lead to a significant change in the structure of the IT market. Although there was traditionally a distinction between hardware and software suppliers, as well as consulting firms (including development and system integration), the spectrum of providers has now clearly expanded and the importance of provider classes for IT departments is shifting.

In future, IT departments will have less and less to do with the classic *providers of hardware*. The use of cloud services renders the issue of server infrastructures obsolete. Even local hardware, such as end-user devices, LANs, or printers are increasingly being purchased as a service, instead of directly from the hardware manufacturer. Similarly, the importance of *standard software providers*, located at on-premise business, will decrease. Instead, there will be an expansion of cloud-based software services (see below).

There will be more *outsourcing providers* in a transitional phase. In the majority of cases, it will not be possible for companies to immediately and completely move their IT infrastructure into the public cloud. However, outsourcing service providers will help them transfer the operations of their own infrastructure. Furthermore, there will always be special architectural domains in certain industries that cannot or may not be covered by generic cloud-based infrastructures (e.g., control systems in power plant operations). In the long term, however, outsourcing providers will lose a significant portion of their business. This will move towards cloud-based software and infrastructure services, as well as managed services (see below).

Software development companies will also continue to exist. In many areas, digitalization will require completely new solutions that cannot be entirely addressed by packaged software or cloud services. In this case, an individual development will continue to be necessary. It is, however, unlikely that the area of individual software development will grow significantly.

Infrastructure-as-a-service provider (IaaS provider) offer basic infrastructure services, such as storage or database solutions and virtual servers. This market segment will experience considerable growth, because, in future, it will cover most of the IT infrastructures in companies. On this basis, *platform-as-a-service providers (PaaS providers)* offer ecosystems that can also include components, such as development tools, generic application functionalities, runtime environments, and also software marketplaces. Platforms have several advantages. Among other things, they can significantly accelerate the software development process, increase the integration capacity of software, and also support easier end-product marketing. As a result, PaaS services are expected to gain considerable importance in future. After all, *software-as-a-service providers* (*SaaS providers*) develop packaged software solutions that end customers can use directly as cloud services. This concept is already widely used at present. Small and medium-sized companies particularly make use of appropriate services, because the software can be provided promptly and often cost-effectively. In addition, no special infrastructure and no IT experts are required for operational and deployment tasks. Furthermore, the SaaS concept can be used to variabilize costs and dynamically call up capacity—depending on actual current demand. Analysts expect SaaS to be the dominant delivery method of the future software world [6].

System integrators configure existing systems and develop custom interfaces between systems to meet customers' specific integration requirements. This will increasingly include the integration of cloud-based solutions (IaaS, PaaS, SaaS). Similarly, *cloud managers* offer complementary services to the above cloud providers, since the very large cloud service providers particularly do not offer any consulting services or services beyond standardized SLAs and terms and conditions, as well as an elementary basic service. For example, there is often no comprehensive help desk or support for configuring cloud services. This is increasingly being done by firms who usually specialize in a few selected large cloud service providers and offer complementary services. In this way, cloud managers "refine" existing cloud services and ensure that they can be used with minimal end-customer involvement. We expect that, in future, there will be *intermediaries* (particularly stock exchanges) that trade in available infrastructure services or capacities.

Based on this suggestion, the IT industry's structure will change significantly. Already now, particularly the major providers are making efforts to position themselves accordingly. Nowadays, all major software firms offer SaaS and, in many cases, PaaS services. In the area of IaaS services, it is already clear who the market leaders will be in the foreseeable future. Examples include Amazon with its web services [7] and Microsoft Azure [8]. Both companies offer a very extensive infrastructure service portfolio from the cloud, which already completely meets the infrastructure needs of many companies. In addition to storage solutions, servers, and database systems, increasingly complex services are on offer, such as big data platforms or systems for machine learning. In their capacity as cloud managers, companies such as TecRacer [9] master these technologies and help companies use them for their own purposes.

On the Way to Cloud Readiness

At present, companies can already prepare themselves for the trends outlined above. Migration towards cloud-based infrastructures and application systems will become much easier if the enterprise architecture is prepared for this change. Such preparation is very important, otherwise existing inefficiencies will be transferred into the cloud-based infrastructure, which will increase consulting, implementation, and later operating costs. The migration may also require technical changes that can already be implemented at present. It will then be possible to decide at a later date when, how, and with whom to execute migration projects. The following design recommendations can be made regardless of specific products, configurations, and providers. If it is not yet feasible to enter the public cloud, these measures can also be used to prepare for the classic outsourcing of in-house IT services.

We recommend that companies should first increase their own infrastructure's degree of virtualization. It is usually much easier to operate virtualized infrastructures on the basis of IaaS services. We therefore recommend that companies investigate the virtualization of their own infrastructure as far as possible and, if feasible, to strive for it. This can also have other positive effects, such as an improved utilization of the companies' own hardware or simplified administration.

Migration to the cloud will also become faster and cheaper if the IT landscape is largely harmonized. This means that as few as possible products or system types are used per hardware and software type. For example, it helps if only one central e-mail system is used and one or two, instead of five, CRM products are used in a corporate environment. IT landscape can be simplified particularly easily in those areas that do not have a differentiating character for the company. Here, any disadvantages of standardization can usually be accepted. However, a much more cautious approach must be taken in differentiated areas in which the loss of competitive advantages can occur if standardization is pushed too far.

In addition to standardizing the systems, a simplification of the systems should also be pursued. This means that the number of systems or system components is reduced as much as possible. In extensive IT environments, it is not uncommon for architectures to be unnecessarily complex or for parts of the architecture to be no longer used. For example, orphaned servers without user activity or unnecessarily complicated network topologies are not uncommon.

In addition, it is possible to check which components of the IT landscape are already "cloud-ready" and which areas still need improvement. A possible improvement can be executed, for example, by replacing non-cloud-compatible software with cloud-compatible software. Basically, one should also ensure that extensions or significant changes to the architecture are only made if they do not complicate or prevent future migration to the cloud. In the context of enterprise architecture management, for example, this can be ensured via appropriate architectural standards and principles.

Preparing (Strategic) Purchasing

The simplification of IT infrastructures based on IaaS, PaaS, and SaaS does not necessarily imply that the purchase of such services becomes easier—on the contrary: Purchasing is becoming more complex and strategic. On the one hand, contracts with service providers are becoming more complex, due to the complexity of service bundles. This is not necessarily the case for highly standardized infrastructure services, but it is certainly true for managed services whereby third-party service bundles are combined, integrated, and monitored. On the other hand, due to an increasing operational and strategic dependency on providers, dedicated relationship management is in most cases of great importance. Monitoring promised service levels, screening the market, price development, and long-term management of the provider portfolio, pose new challenges for IT purchasing. Here, one can and should take early action. Corresponding processes, structures, regulations, and responsibilities must be defined, tested, and institutionalized at an early stage. In this way, the risks associated with the external service procurement can be minimized.

> **Overview: Infrastructure as a Commodity**
> - In future, the non-differentiating elements of IT landscapes will be sourced from the cloud.
> - The reason for this is that today's data processing center operations are based on assumptions that are predominantly no longer valid.
> - Cloud-based IT landscapes will therefore become significantly more important in future.
> - Standardization at all levels of the company architecture is a key driver of this development.
> - As a result, the scope of providers in the IT market will change significantly.
> - Traditional hardware and software providers are losing importance; IaaS, PaaS, and SaaS providers are become more important.
> - New specialized vendors that can plan, implement, integrate, and manage cloud-based IT landscapes will gain importance.
> - Companies are well advised to prepare themselves for this development; strategic IT purchasing faces new challenges.

References

1. Wheatley, M. (2016, January 18). A third of all IT infrastructure spending now goes to the cloud. *siliconANGLE*. http://siliconangle.com/blog/2016/01/18/a-third-of-all-it-infrastructure-spending-now-goes-to-the-cloud/?es_p=1194290
2. Carr, N. (2003, May 5–12). IT doesn't matter. *Harvard Business Review*.
3. Bundesamt für Sicherheit in der Informationstechnik. (2014). *IT-Grundschutz-Kataloge*. https://www.bsi.bund.de/DE/Themen/ITGrundschutz/ITGrundschutzKataloge/itgrundschutzkataloge_node.html

4. Deutsche Börse Cloud Exchange AG. https://cloud.exchange/
5. Herrmann, W. (2016, February 10). Deutsche Börse Cloud Exchange gibt auf. *CIO*. http://www.cio.de/a/deutsche-boerse-cloud-exchange-gibt-auf,3253713
6. Praxmarer, L., & Peichert, L. (2015, December 9). Die wichtigsten IT-Trends für 2016. *CIO*. http://www.cio.de/a/die-wichtigsten-it-trends-fuer-2016,3251266
7. https://aws.amazon.com
8. https://azure.microsoft.com
9. https://www.tecracer.de/

Digitalization as a Risk: Security and Business Continuity Management Are Central Cross-Divisional Functions of the Company

Digital transformation's essential characteristic is the innovative use of information technologies with direct business benefits for the company. As we have already pointed out repeatedly in this book, the digitalization of the business world offers numerous opportunities through IT-based value creation, as well as product and business model innovations. However, even in this context, the benefits are not without associated risks. With an increasing diffusion of information technology, companies in the digital world are more and more dependent on the availability of their IT systems. The easy accessibility of systems via the Internet also leads to increased vulnerability. Accordingly, IT security is becoming the "ugly sister of digitalization," as Ralf Schneider, Group CIO of Allianz, expressed at the Hamburg IT Strategy Days in early 2016 [1].

Depending on the sector and business model (e.g., banks or stock exchanges), a system no longer available can already mean the end for the affected company. Furthermore, the advent of information technology in products and services will also increasingly influence the physical well-being of individuals—such as self-driving cars, robots in the care sector, and autonomous control systems in power plants. However, in our opinion many companies still underestimate IT risks that are often not fully controlled. One of the main reasons for this is that IT security problems currently have limited scope and many managers are not yet sufficiently aware of this. However, we observe, with increasing severity, that effective IT security and business continuity management are becoming central competencies for sustainable business activity, which should be organized as cross-divisional functions within a company. Developing security skills is, thus, becoming an important task of digital business.

© Springer International Publishing AG, part of Springer Nature 2019
N. Urbach, F. Ahlemann, *IT Management in the Digital Age*, Management for Professionals, https://doi.org/10.1007/978-3-319-96187-3_9

Current IT Security Risks Are Mostly of Limited Scope

IT security is already an integral part of IT governance in the majority of companies, and is managed by dedicated individuals, such as the chief information security officer (CISO). The importance of IT security and corresponding security guidelines is regularly emphasized—especially when, once again, the press publishes horror reports of virus infections or other Internet-based attacks. Although the importance of IT security in companies has increased in recent years [2], a closer investigation at companies creates the impression that the topic still plays a rather minor role and that the increased—and increasing—importance of information technology in the business context is not sufficiently taken into account. IT risks are significantly underestimated by many companies and are not fully managed in the event of an emergency. A similar assessment is also made in a survey of 200 CIOs and CTOs in Germany [3]. As a result of the study, business leaders often do not consider the dangers for their own IT. A total of 46% of the study participants stated that senior management did not give IT security problems any priority. At the same time, 43% of the respondents found an increased number of security incidents. Similar conclusions can also be drawn from a study commissioned by the German Federal Ministry of Economics and Technology on the IT security level in small and medium-sized enterprises (SMEs) [4]. According to the results of the study, the IT security level of SMEs in Germany apparently needs considerable improvement against a background of information technology being highly significant for the economy. Although a high awareness concerning the relevance of IT security and a certain level of technical measures has been achieved almost everywhere. The research findings show, however, that there is a lack of organizational and staff-related measures. The findings also show that there is a lack of insight that incidents in the IT area can permanently disrupt elementary business processes, that IT security routines must be established, and that defined emergency procedures must be put in place.

In the majority of cases, the often still neglected approach to IT security has not yet led to major problems. The main reason for this is that the IT security problems that occur, are usually of limited scope for companies. On the one hand, in many cases the extent of damage is manageable. On the other hand, a failure of IT components for a few days can still be tolerated relatively well. However, there are already companies and industries for which even small IT failures can become a business-critical threat. The obvious examples are online companies, as well as banks and stock exchanges, for which a failure of parts of the IT infrastructure will have significant economic implications—up to and including the end of business activities. Similarly, such failures in critical infrastructures, for example in the areas of energy supply or health care, can have direct risks for the population.

Marc Elsberg describes an appropriate horror scenario in his novel, "Blackout," [5] which is well worth reading. In this fictitious case, all electricity grids collapse throughout Europe, due to hacker attacks. As a consequence, public life comes to a complete standstill and civil war-like conditions break out. The majority of IT security risks will not necessarily have such effects. However, the attacks by ransomware

"Locky" have already shown what damage can be caused solely by "simple virus attacks." At peak times, more than 5000 new infections per hour were recorded in Germany alone [6]. As a result, several hospitals were only partially functional for a few days, because many systems had to be shut down [7].

The Threats Are Becoming More Diverse

The ubiquitous nature of the Internet, the ever-increasing spread of information technology, and the increasing interconnectedness of systems mean that the threat situation is indeed increasing. For a long time, it was necessary to protect oneself "only" against malware—especially viruses—but presently there are completely new security-related challenges, some of which should be outlined here.

Perhaps the best-known threat comes from the *malware* mentioned above, which is not targeted at individual companies or users, but can nevertheless cause considerable disruption to IT operations. This particularly includes virus software that gains control of computer systems, which can lead to direct data loss. The virus protection programs, which have been available for many years, help protect against such threats to a certain extent—provided that these systems are regularly updated.

Internet-based fraud and economic crime have experienced considerable growth in recent years. It is particularly noteworthy that the level of organized crime has increased significantly in this area. A characteristic feature of the associated threat is that individuals or gangs try to gain access to important corporate resources (usually funds). They use a variety of methods, ranging from sending phishing mails to compromising entire corporate infrastructures. Often, this is done very professionally. Certain criminals, for example, try to get access to systems via company employees. Examples include sending highly personalized—and therefore credible—phishing mails or trying to establish personal relationships with employees. There is a reported case where the intruders, pretending to be representatives of a security company, were introduced to an accountant and asked him to log on to the SAP system for security checks. They could, thus, create payment instructions and, later on, use fake e-mails to persuade managers to authorize them.

And then there is also the danger of an *attack from the inside*. Frustrated, disappointed, or criminal employees can behave in a destructive manner and harm the company by deleting data, destroying systems, or initiating business transactions that are not in the company's interest. It is especially difficult for a company to defend itself against such attacks; it requires a mature access management system and IT resources with reliable security.

Presumably the problem of *cyber-terrorism* will become more relevant in the coming years. It is not a question of attacking an individual company, but of harming a state, a region, or a specific part of society whereby the perpetrators aim to assert their own political or religious interests. Thus far, the Federal Republic of Germany has not been the victim of widespread cyber-terrorist attacks, but it cannot be ruled out for the future. Companies may be directly or indirectly affected by such attacks. A direct effect occurs when the focus is on the company's own IT infrastructure or applications. Indirect effects occur when critical (public) infrastructures are affected and the exchange of services with other organizations is impaired. This is the case, for example, when logistics processes no longer function, due to an attack on transport systems, or when energy can no longer be purchased, because power plants have been attacked and are no longer functional.

Many companies are already afraid of *industrial espionage*, and they have already fallen victim to it. In 2015, for example, the Bitkom digital association published a study showing that more than half of the participating companies have fallen victim to digital industrial espionage, sabotage, or data theft in the last 2 years. According to the results, the most vulnerable sector is the automotive industry, followed by chemical and pharmaceutical industries, as well as banks and insurance companies. According to Bitkom's conservative calculations, the damage caused to the entire German economy amounts to approximately 51 billion euros per year. A quarter of this amount results from a loss of revenue, due to plagiarism. This is followed—in third position—by patent right infringements, as well as losses in turnover, due to the loss of competitive advantages [8].

Last but not least, it must be pointed out that many security-related incidents in companies are not the result of inadequate technical protection measures, but rather the result of human misconduct. The best passwords are of no assistance if they are disclosed or written on notes that stuck to the monitor. The redundant design of critical infrastructure and the best firewalls are useless when security and supervisory staff fail to deny unauthorized access to the data center. Purely technical security of the company will therefore not be sufficient to protect itself against dangers.

Secure and Stable IT Becomes a Business-Critical Resource

Digitalization—at the very least—makes secure and stable IT a business-critical resource. IT security incidents will therefore no longer only cause an impairment for most companies, but can also have potentially damaging effects on business. Since the processing of personal data is becoming increasingly important in the digital economy, data security and data protection is also becoming more important. Problems of this kind can lead to customers and business partners losing much confidence, which can also have business-critical implications. In 2015, for example, the Canadian subsidiary of the U.S. retail chain, Target, went bankrupt after a hacker stole 40 million records of credit and bank card data, including the PIN codes and data of 70 million customers. Many customers avoided the shops after the hacker attack, because they no longer trusted credit card payments to be secure and many Canadian consumers did not consider cash payments as an alternative [9].

However, digitalization does not only make IT security more important for business. By introducing IT into digital products and services, the physical well-being of individuals can also be affected in the event of damage. The Internet of things, for example, intervenes more and more in our everyday world with an increasing number of actuators and sensors. Previously "non-critical systems" are increasingly classified as mission-critical. Here, the obvious examples are self-driving automobiles, robots in the care sector, or autonomous control systems for power plants. Disruptions in autonomous robots that work together with human operators in production processes, or that work in sensitive infrastructures, such as rail transport, can also have devastating consequences.

Development of Security Competencies for the Digital Business

In the context of increasing IT penetration in the business context, IT security and business continuity management are becoming central competencies for sustainable business operations. On the one hand, this involves proactively dealing with potential IT security risks to keep the probability of their occurrence as low as possible. On the other hand, the continuation of business operations must be ensured in the event of failure. Due to the clearly increasing scope of IT security risks, approaches that go far beyond the usual current implementations become necessary. In addition to classic security analyses that focus on data protection and security, as well as failure and dependency analyses that focus on the continuation of business activities, in future it will be a matter of protecting people, organizations, and society from autonomous systems with malfunctions of any kind. The risk potential increases more than proportionately to the extent that systems are interconnected, become more autonomous and intelligent, and humans become more dependent on them. The reason for this disproportionate increase is that a large number of security risks have to be considered with every network and every autonomous, intelligent component [10].

The increasing interconnectedness creates a higher access potential for many and, thus, a higher probability of attacks. For example, the possibility of connecting machines to the Internet means that these devices can be accessed worldwide for maintenance purposes. It is, of course, important that not everyone should be able to access a configuration interface, but only a certain group of people. Security mechanisms are therefore essential to combine the advantages of Internet connectivity—regardless of time or location—with the limitation of access. However, increased interconnectedness also increases the damage potential of a security attack. An attack on an office employee's personal computer, for example, not only has an impact on the office employee's personal computer, but can, for example, also affect the control of machines in production. The consequences are obvious: The more interactive and interconnected the systems become, the more extensive—thus, also greater—the damage becomes that can be caused by safety failures.

Simultaneously, it becomes increasingly difficult to identify and understand the error potentials, because of the highly interconnected and, thus, very complex systems. We are already noticing an increasing susceptibility to errors in systems that have been significantly more error-free in the past. A realistic, everyday example is the car. Here, the development of the past few years resulted in increasingly better fitted and safer cars. At the same time, these technical upgrades have made cars more complex and more susceptible to errors. For example, a study by the Center of Automotive Management shows that, more than 45 million cars—in the USA alone—were recalled in 2015, because of safety problems. Compared to the number of vehicles sold on the American market in the same period, this means that two and a half times more vehicles were affected by recalls [11]. In recent years, corporate IT also underwent a similar development—we only need to consider the growing and extremely complex IT architectures in most companies. A stronger infiltration of information technology into products and services in the digital transformation context will probably reinforce this trend rather than reduce it.

IT Security as a Task for the Entire Company

The development of a comprehensive IT security management system is key for companies that want to be prepared for digital transformation. This aims at ensuring the IT security of the company in an ongoing process and, thus, keeping the probability of IT security incidents and the extent of the potential damage as low as possible. German politicians have already recognized the special need for comprehensive IT protection and since mid-2015 it has been addressed by the "Act to Increase the Security of Information Technology Systems"—better known as the "IT Security Act." Amongst others, the Act stipulates that operators of critical infrastructures must, above all else, adhere to a minimum level of IT security and report IT security incidents to the Federal Office for Information Security (BSI) [12]. The implementation of a basic IT security management system is not difficult, because standards and regulations have already been established. In this way, standards, such as ISO 27001, and the BSI's recommendations can form a good basis [13].

It will not be possible to implement a comprehensive and functioning IT security management system if there is not sufficient transparency about the infrastructure and application landscape's architecture. For this reason, at least rudimentary architecture management is a mandatory prerequisite for IT security management. The IT landscape must at least be documented and evaluated regarding security aspects. This means that architectural components must be classified according to their protection requirements. This, in turn, requires the development and implementation of security concepts that meet the protection requirements.

However, since the best IT security concept cannot guarantee complete security, we predict the establishment of effective business continuity management as a further operational area. This involves ensuring the continued existence of the company in the event of a crisis, which, in the case of digital business, primarily (although not exclusively) concerns the continuation of information technology operations. In order to achieve this, companies must identify all critical business processes in the course of a risk analysis. The next step is to set up an emergency management system for these critical processes. For example, the Federal Office for Security and Information Technology (BSI) provides a guideline—with the BSI Standard 100-4—on how such business continuity management can be structured [14].

In the majority of companies, IT security and business continuity management are primarily understood as tasks of corporate IT. Accordingly, security awareness seems to be lower in the business areas than in the IT department. For example, IBM recently conducted a study with the participation of 5200 IT decision-makers. The study shows that 76% of the CIOs who were surveyed, consider IT security to be a critical success factor for digitalization, but only 67% of the CxOs who were surveyed, consider it to be a critical factor for success [15]. However, due to the increasing importance of secure and stable IT for the entire company in the digital transformation context, the topic of IT security should no longer be regarded as only being an IT concern. Instead, it should be understood and practiced as a task of the entire company. In order to raise the IT security level sustainably, it is necessary for corporate management to recognize IT security as strategically relevant. This is the only way in which to give the IT department the necessary authority and financial resources, as well as the necessary political backing, to be able to implement appropriate measures within the company. In our opinion, this is also important, because the majority of the IT dangers arise internally—from the employees themselves. Only when IT security is recognized as a strategic corporate task, will employees develop a sensitivity to this topic. Accordingly, IT security and business continuity management should no longer be the pure responsibility of corporate IT, but should be organized as a cross-functional function of the entire company.

As soon as a company has established a coherent security concept, sensitized and trained its employees, and implemented modern security technologies, the highest possible level of security no longer needs to be regarded as a stumbling block, but can be regarded as a genuine competitive advantage [16]. Internally, appropriate solutions can be considered particularly good if they are barely noticed, but effectively and efficiently prevent attacks in the background, and ensure that business operations continue in an emergency. However, strong IT security management can, when successful, also have an external impact and contribute to the reputation of the digital company.

Overview: Digitalization as a Risk
- IT security plays a minor role in a number of companies.
- Presently, IT security risks are usually only of limited scope.
- Digitalization is turning secure and stable IT into a business-critical resource.
- IT security incidents can increasingly endanger business.
- With the introduction of IT in products and services, the physical well-being of individuals can also be increasingly affected in the event of damage.
- The development of security competencies is becoming an important digital transformation task.
- IT security and business continuity management are organized as a cross-divisional function of the company.

References

1. Hülsbömer, S. (2016, February 18). IT-Sicherheit – Die hässliche Schwester der Digitalisierung. *CIO*. http://www.cio.de/a/it-sicherheit-die-haessliche-schwester-der-digitalisierung,3253997
2. Ziemann, F. (2011, September 2). 2011 State of Security Survey: Bedeutung der IT-Sicherheit in Unternehmen steigt. *PC Welt*. http://www.pcwelt.de/news/Bedeutung-der-IT-Sicherheit-in-Unternehmen-steigt-3402089.html
3. Robert Half Technology. (2014, December 1). *Studie: Jede zweite Führungskraft unterschätzt Cyber-Security*. https://www.roberthalf.de/presse/studie-jede-zweite-fuehrungskraft-unterschaetzt-cyber-security
4. Bundesministeriums für Wirtschaft und Technologie. (2012, September). *IT-Sicherheitsniveau in kleinen und mittleren Unternehmen*. https://www.bmwi.de/BMWi/Redaktion/PDF/S-T/studie-it-sicherheit,property=pdf,bereich=bmwi2012,sprache=de,rwb=true.pdf
5. Elsberg, M. (2013). *BLACKOUT – Morgen ist es zu spät*. München: Blanvalet Taschenbuch Verlag.
6. Eikenberg, H. (2016, February 19). Krypto-Trojaner Locky wütet in Deutschland: Über 5000 Infektionen pro Stunde. *heise online*. http://www.heise.de/security/meldung/Krypto-Trojaner-Locky-wuetet-in-Deutschland-Ueber-5000-Infektionen-pro-Stunde-3111774.html
7. Borchers, D. (2016, February 12). Ransomware-Virus legt Krankenhaus lahm. *heise online*. http://www.heise.de/newsticker/meldung/Ransomware-Virus-legt-Krankenhaus-lahm-3100418.html
8. Bitkom. (2015, April 16). *Digitale Angriffe auf jedes zweite Unternehmen*. https://www.bitkom.org/Presse/Presseinformation/Digitale-Angriffe-auf-jedes-zweite-Unternehmen.html
9. Sokolov, D. (2015, February 13). Ein Jahr nach Datenleck: Target Kanada ist Pleite. *heise online*. http://www.heise.de/tp/artikel/44/44121/1.html
10. Groß, H. (2013, June). *Industrie 4.0 – Vernetzung braucht IT-Sicherheit*. Lancom Systems. https://www.lancom-systems.de/download/documentation/Whitepaper/Studie_Industrie_4.0_v3.pdf
11. CIO. (2016, January 15). Studie: Technische Aufrüstung macht Autos immer fehleranfälliger. *CIO*. http://www.cio.de/a/technische-aufruestung-macht-autos-immer-fehleranfaelliger,3221838
12. Bundesministerium des Innern. (2015, July 17). *Gesetz zur Erhöhung der Sicherheit informationstechnischer Systeme (IT-Sicherheitsgesetz)*. https://www.bmi.bund.de/SharedDocs/Downloads/DE/Gesetzestexte/it-sicherheitsgesetz
13. Bundesamt für Sicherheit in der Informationstechnik (o.J.). *ISO 27001 Zertifizierung auf Basis von IT-Grundschutz*. https://www.bsi.bund.de/DE/Themen/ZertifizierungundAnerkennung/Managementsystemzertifizierung/Zertifizierung27001/GS_Zertifizierung_node.html
14. Bundesamt für Sicherheit in der Informationstechnik. (2008). *BSI-Standard 100-4 – Nofallmanagement, Version 1.0*. https://www.bsi.bund.de/SharedDocs/Downloads/DE/BSI/Publikationen/ITGrundschutzstandards/standard_1004_pdf.pdf?__blob=publicationFile
15. Pütter, C. (2016, 17 März). Stellschrauben der Digitalisierung: Wo CIOs daneben liegen. *CIO*. http://www.cio.de/a/wo-cios-daneben-liegen,3255180
16. Schasche, S. (2015, September 17). IT-Sicherheit ist von strategischer Bedeutung. *Computerwoche*. http://www.computerwoche.de/a/it-sicherheit-ist-von-strategischer-bedeutung,3216059

Transformable IT Landscapes: IT Architectures Are Standardized, Modular, Flexible, Ubiquitous, Elastic, Cost-Effective, and Secure

Current IT architectures are often very complex—usually much more complex than they should be. A large number of technologies, products, proprietary developments, configurations, and interfaces converge to form a larger whole, which a single person can hardly fathom. Thousands of business application systems are often used in large corporate structures. There are telecommunication, production, logistics, and other systems. The consequences are obvious and clear to every IT manager. Dynamic adjustments are difficult, risky, expensive, and time-consuming. However, in times of digitalization it should be the other way around: simple, with manageable risk, inexpensive, and fast. This can only be achieved with a highly standardized, modular, flexible, ubiquitous, and elastic IT architecture. The goal is "modular IT," which enables fast, easy implementation of new solutions through the uncomplicated integration of existing modules.

Laborious Consolidation and Standardization of the IT Architecture

Historically, the current complexity of many IT architectures is relatively easy to explain. For decades, business requirements were covered by the development of monolithic individual systems (silos). Integration requirements were not at the heart of the respective projects. The result is a low level of integration depth, which is noticeable, for example, through media discontinuities, poor data quality, or high maintenance costs. In order to meet these challenges, more and more interfaces were developed, but they did not follow a unified overall concept. The consequence was point-to-point connections based on completely different paradigms and protocols. In addition, there was a very high technological diversity due to a large number of technology providers and generally low standardization within the IT industry.

Initial attempts to meet these challenges were often unsuccessful. For example, the idea of developing company data models and using them as a basis for the

© Springer International Publishing AG, part of Springer Nature 2019   93
N. Urbach, F. Ahlemann, *IT Management in the Digital Age*, Management for Professionals, https://doi.org/10.1007/978-3-319-96187-3_10

(further) development of information systems, has not been successful in most cases. The use of large standard software systems for ERP, CRM, or SCM helped many companies mitigate integration challenges. In many cases, however, the price of less successful or completely failed implementation projects and rampant configuration requirements was paid over and over again.

Even today, many organizations still suffer from their far too complex IT architectures. The consequences are indeed complex: Without suitable countermeasures, there is a loss of transparency and, as a result, increased risks and complexity costs, as well as decreasing flexibility and also decreasing speed in the implementation of new solutions. All in all, this can impair the ability to successfully implement new (digital) strategies.

Approaches to Reduce Complexity

In order to overcome these challenges, science and practice developed a number of approaches. *Standardization* is intended to make the IT landscape more uniform—in principle [1]. This involves the reduction of technological, product, and process diversity (see chapter "Infrastructure as commodity: IT infrastructure services are traded on free markets and purchased as required"). Standardization is supported by market consolidation trends in almost all sectors, as well as the development of industry standards and norms. However, "internal standardization" is also required. This involves the survey and analysis of the IT landscape, as well as the points at which there is an excessive—unnecessary—diversity of technologies, products, and processes. For example, the number of database management systems, operating systems, development platforms, or instances of an application system, can be reduced in this way.

The enterprise architecture management (EAM) approach is similar, but more comprehensive, in that it aims to further develop the IT landscape (and increasingly also the business processes) in the direction of a desired target state by means of targeted analysis, planning, and implementation processes [2]. The necessary changes are usually long-term and require strategic commitment. Unfortunately, many EAM initiatives do not have the desired effect. This is often due to the fact that the architects involved with EAM do not have the necessary influence and decision-making powers. In addition, it is crucial to choose an EAM approach that suits the organization and the existing IT landscape. For example, it is not very promising to try and capture very large, complex IT landscapes completely in the form of models, and to develop a target architecture on the basis of complete information. Many IT architectures are too complex and too dynamic for this, to the extent that collecting the relevant data, in itself, would be too costly.

The more specialized approaches, such as data quality [3] and master data management [4], are closely linked to architecture management. They respond to the problem of data integrity, availability, and keeping data updated. The first approach is about systematically improving data quality through dedicated processes, rules, architectural principles, and responsibilities across the application boundaries. The latter involves a centralized and systematic management of master data, which is often one of the most important data stocks in a company. Both approaches are similar, overlap, and have become particularly widespread in recent years, especially in large companies.

Unsurprisingly, the technology providers created solutions that are designed to reduce the IT landscape's complexity, thereby enabling it to become operational again. These include service-oriented architectures (SOAs) [5], development platforms, and development frameworks. The basic idea is simple and plausible. Instead of meeting integration requirements with individual point-to-point interfaces, systems offer a uniform set of open interfaces that are shared by all neighboring systems. This leads to a considerable reduction of the number of interfaces. In addition, it entails the standardization of interface technology (via the Simple Object Access Protocol, SOAP) and complex hub-oriented transport systems (Enterprise Service Bus, ESB), which involve aspects, such as encryption, authentication, or message transport, in complex network topologies. The consistent use of SOA not only reduces the complexity of the interface architecture; it also ensures a higher degree of reuse. SOA does not only allow the exchange of data between systems. Instead, functionalities of other systems can also be used by remote procedure calls (RPC). SOA and related advanced concepts are increasingly supported by development platforms and frameworks. This reduces training and implementation efforts on the part of software developers and accelerates development processes. The SOA concept has been put into practice, but has not been widely disseminated, as was predicted a few years ago. It is widely used in the banking and insurance sectors, in particular. This is not surprising, because individual developments still dominate in many cases and the integration requirements are particularly challenging. For example, ING-DiBa pursues a strategy in terms whereof the reuse of code and existing solutions are maximized via open interfaces, thereby enabling it to develop customer-oriented solutions more quickly [6].

The SOA concept and the corresponding technologies have undergone continuous further development. Currently, so-called micro services are also being discussed [7]. These are very fine-granular software functions that are offered via open services. They can be connected quickly and easily to implement more complex systems or to support processes. Micro services are based on the understanding that a variety of simple services are easier to maintain and that the degree of reuse increases. It is not yet possible to say conclusively whether the concept will gain acceptance on a broad front.

All in all, it can be said that many companies are still in a process of architectural optimization and that many actual architectures are only conditionally prepared for the requirements of digitalization. Although the approaches outlined above are worthwhile, by themselves they will not be sufficient to meet the requirements of digitalization.

Future IT Landscapes Must Be Easy to Transform

Digital transformation makes special demands on IT architectures for various technical and business reasons. On the technical side, the use of new technologies can be expected. Trends such as the *Internet of things* or *Industry 4.0* are leading to the emergence of completely new device classes that need to be integrated into existing infrastructures. In many cases, however, consolidation and standardization processes have not yet taken place here. We can therefore expect a significant increase in the complexity of the architectures. Furthermore, from a business point of view, it is also necessary that digital innovations can be implemented quickly and easily to survive in the face of competition. The following characteristics of future IT architectures are derived from the above-described standardization.

The most fundamental requirement concerns the *modularity*. The design of the overall architecture should be based on self-contained, individual components that can be used through defined interfaces. However, the components' internal functionality will be hidden. This reduces complexity and allows an isolated, further development of the components. At the same time, the existing components can be combined, as needed, to meet new business needs. This will result in multiple use ("re-use"), which will reduce development efforts and accelerate development processes. Although the idea of modularity is comparatively old, it is perhaps the most important prerequisite for "modular IT." It originates from the early days of software engineering and forms the basis of many current solution architectures.

Modular IT architecture can only fully exploit its advantages if it is highly flexible. This means that arbitrary components from different manufacturers can be combined with each other on the basis of arbitrary products in order to increase the integration and easily comply with new requirements. This only works if the interfaces are standardized and based on uniform technologies. The standardization of interfaces entails two aspects. On the one hand, interfaces needs to be harmonized syntactically, which means that they need to use the same protocols and data formats. For example, a company can decide to use either SOAP based on hypertext transfer protocol secured (HTTPS), or a specific ESB. On the other hand, a semantic harmonization need to be achieved, which can refer to the definition of business objects, the meaning of data fields, and certain business rules. An example is the supply chain operations reference (SCOR) model, which specifies internal and cross-company supply chain management processes [8].

Future IT architectures will be ubiquitous in the sense that they will be available everywhere—that is, globally. On the one hand, this can be achieved by a carefully planned redundant design of the systems. In this case, the problem associated with redundant data retention, downstream consistency, and updates has to be solved. Alternatively, existing WANs can be used to make the architecture available. In the vast majority of cases, it will be advisable to use the Internet or virtual networks based on the Internet. Furthermore, ubiquitous also means that the architecture support all relevant devices. This implies a strict separation of business logic and input/output, and leads to layered software models, which are already commonplace at present. Many companies already demand that all application systems should use web-based front ends. The advantage of this is that all end device classes are supported and its positive side effect is that the deployment of an application is no longer a problem.

After all, the *elasticity* of future IT architectures needs to be demanded. This means that capacities can be dynamically built up and reduced according to demand in order to achieve a variabilization of IT costs. In this context, one should particularly mention architectures based on public cloud offerings, such as infrastructure-as-a-service (IaaS). The particular advantage of cloud services is that several customers can simultaneously use IT resources. This avoids peak loads and results in a more even utilization of available IT resources (see chapter "Infrastructure as commodity: IT infrastructure services are traded on free markets and purchased as required").

Closely linked to elasticity is the requirement that IT architectures should be cost-effective. This is particularly noticeable in the context of the often too high complexity costs resulting from architectures that consist of too many individual elements, which, in turn, are highly diverse. Approaches to reduce complexity (see above) can help here. In times of digitalization, a low-cost IT system will have a major impact on a cost-effective value chain in more and more companies and can therefore be decisive for competition in future. It is not by accident that many companies are already conducting benchmarking projects to check whether they have competitive IT cost structures not only compared to similar companies in their industry, but also compared to external outsourcing service providers and public cloud providers. The increasing degree of standardization in IT facilitates cost comparisons.

The increasing dependency of companies on information technology, combined with new threats, requires a secure IT architecture. Legislators are already demanding this at present and will continue to do so in future. The concept of security is becoming ever more comprehensive. It is no longer only about protecting data. In the time of the Internet of things with sensors and actuators and the ever-expanding integration of IT in all areas of life, the immediate well-being of individuals or groups of people—including society as a whole—can depend on the security of information technology. For example, robots that interact directly with humans can become dangerous if they are controlled by malicious programs (see chapter "Digitalization as a risk: security and business continuity management are central cross-divisional functions of the company").

Many of the requirements described above can practically only be met by (public) cloud concepts. Modularity, flexibility, and ubiquity are inherent in every comprehensive cloud service. Internal employees are usually no better at ensuring secure architectures than public cloud services experts. On the contrary: For many companies, the recruitment of security experts is currently a bigger challenge than ever before. The cost of public cloud services is also acceptable to many companies. Although a profit margin has to be paid, economies of scale usually ensure that internally provided services will not be cheaper or will only be insignificantly cheaper. From a cost perspective, it therefore only makes sense for large and very large IT departments to provide their own services. Here, possible economies of scale can be achieved. The outsourcing of IT architecture components to the public cloud also solves another problem: The shortage of skilled professionals can be effectively counteracted in this way.

Functioning Architecture Management as a Central Prerequisite

A functioning architecture management can be understood as a central prerequisite for the development of sustainable IT architectures and the initiation of corresponding migration projects. Especially for medium to large IT environments, it helps create the necessary transparency to prepare, plan, and execute appropriate migrations. It should be noted that, in the majority of cases, it makes no sense to move an existing architecture into a (public) cloud or to replace it with cloud-based services without changing it. In the majority of cases, the opportunity is missed to reduce unnecessary complexity, thereby resulting in the cloud-based architecture becoming more expensive than necessary, or having speed and stability problems. It may also be necessary to make adjustments, because not all architectural elements are cloud-compatible. For these reasons, we recommend that migration to the cloud is preceded by a comprehensive optimization program that reduces (a) unnecessary complexity and (b) examines the feasibility of cloud migration with regard to all (relevant) architectural components. Optimization and preparation can even affect business processes or organizational structures, namely whenever (a) business functions arise, due to changes at the application system level, (b) the analyses show that the complexity is caused by excessively and not necessarily complex business processes, or (c) service production processes in the IT department change due to cloud migration.

This optimization program can be understood as an architecture management initiative that is usually initiated and controlled by company architects. In order for this to work, architects must be given clear strategic objectives, as well as sufficient decision-making powers and veto rights. Our own empirical studies also prove that it is advantageous for a top manager to take over the "supervision" of the architectural transformation. He or she serves as an escalation authority, provides the necessary resources, and supports change management. In order to ensure that the architecture is further developed in accordance with the long-term goals and to avoid a renewed increase in complexity, architectural principles and standards must be defined and serve as "guidelines" for the further development of IT. It is also important to understand that the positive effects of such an architecture management system are only realized in the long term. Optimization is an investment in the future. Initially, it costs a lot of money and the positive effects are often indirect and difficult to assess in monetary terms.

As soon as this optimization program has been completed, cloud migration can be carried out gradually or in individual steps for large IT architectures. At the same time, it is important to establish a functioning provider management system. This ensures that cloud providers fulfill their obligations and that a long-term productive cooperation becomes possible.

Overview: Transformable IT Landscapes
- In the majority of cases, the current IT landscapes of companies do not yet meet the requirements of digitalization.
- Previous optimization approaches, such as the consolidation of application portfolios or service-oriented architectures, will not be sufficient to support digitalization.
- Future architectures will have to be standardized, modular, flexible, ubiquitous, elastic, cost-effective, and secure.
- In order to achieve these goals in the long term, many companies will not be able to escape the public cloud.
- Already today, companies can prepare a gradual migration by means of targeted architecture management.

References

1. Dittes, S., Urbach, N., & Ahlemann, F. (2014). IT-Standardisierung—Vom Lippenbekenntnis zu nachhaltigem Nutzen. *Wirtschaftsinformatik and Management, 6*(4), 29–39.
2. Ahlemann, F., Stettiner, E., Messerschmidt, M., & Legner, C. (2012). *Strategic enterprise architecture management: Challenges, best practices, and future developments*. Heidelberg: Springer Science & Business Media.
3. Otto, B., & Österle, H. (2015). *Corporate data quality: Voraussetzung erfolgreicher Geschäftsmodelle*. Berlin: Springer Gabler.
4. Scheuch, R., Gansor, T., & Ziller, C. (2012). *Master data management: Strategie, Organisation, Architektur*. Heidelberg: dpunkt.verlag.
5. Starke, G., & Tilkov, S. (2007). *SOA-Expertenwissen: Methoden, Konzepte und Praxis serviceorientierter Architekturen*. Heidelberg: dpunkt.verlag.
6. Lixenfeld, C. (2015, July 9). Keine IT-Abteilung mehr nötig: Die Digitalstrategie der ING-Diba. *CIO*. http://www.cio.de/a/die-digitalstrategie-der-ing-diba,3109668
7. Wolff, E. (2015). *Microservices: Grundlagen flexibler Softwarearchitekturen*. Heidelberg: dpunkt.verlag.
8. Bolstorff, P. A., Rosenbaum, R. G., & Poluha, R. G. (2007). *Spitzenleistungen im Supply Chain Management—Ein Praxishandbuch zur Optimierung mit SCOR*. Berlin: Springer.

The End of the IT Department: IT Experts Become Part of the Business Departments and Are Coordinated by a Dedicated Executive Responsibility

In view of the developments described in the preceding chapters, it is obvious that the question of how IT departments will be structured in future and where they will be organizationally anchored, is already asked today. There are a number of indications that IT departments, as we currently know them today, will not survive. If more and more tasks are carried out in the immediate vicinity of the business units or directly in the business units (see chapters "Development and operation are not decisive: IT management follows the "innovate-design-transform" paradigm" and "Focusing on the user: development processes are agile, end-user-centered, and merged with the operation"), if large parts of the IT value chain are carried out externally (see chapters "Infrastructure as commodity: IT infrastructure services are traded on free markets and purchased as required" and "Transformable IT landscapes: IT architectures are standardized, modular, flexible, ubiquitous, elastic, cost-effective, and secure") and if, simultaneously, IT receives more strategic attention than ever before (see chapters "The digital revolution: how technological trends change the business world" and "No business without IT: IT is the central and indispensable driver of entrepreneurial value creation"), then—from our point of view—the current IT department, located on the second or third management level is very poorly positioned for the digital transformation. We are of the opinion that the classic IT department has become obsolete and that the remaining tasks of corporate IT are better suited for a central function, which—in view of the ever-increasing importance of information technology for the company as a whole—should be anchored close to the executive board.

The Classic IT Department in Crisis

Current IT departments base their principles on the "plan-build-run" paradigm. Accordingly, structures and processes are aligned to the three main tasks of planning, development, and operation. "Plan" means recording the business departments' basic requirements. It is a question of which IT services are needed according to what

© Springer International Publishing AG, part of Springer Nature 2019

N. Urbach, F. Ahlemann, *IT Management in the Digital Age*, Management for Professionals, https://doi.org/10.1007/978-3-319-96187-3_11

quality and quantity. This is followed by deriving an IT investment portfolio, which is necessary to implement the necessary changes in the IT value chain. However, it is also about the systematic further development of the IT department within the boundaries of the plan-build-run paradigm. "Build" encompasses all project and line activities to expand or change the service portfolio or the value chain. Here, for example, new systems are developed or IT management processes are optimized. In the "run" context, the IT services are provided, this means that they are made available to the business units. This includes, for example, running an operational data processing center and handling support processes for users.

IT departments have been optimizing and automating these basic processes for many years—to such an extent that they talk about the "industrialization of IT," which is accompanied by an increasing functional specialization and automation within the IT department. The result, for example, was shared service companies within corporate structures that often work efficiently, but are no longer perceived by the business units as equal partners. This is not surprising: In addition to the often significant physical distance, the different technical languages and cultures, and also—often—the lack of business-related knowledge on the part of the IT experts, lead to a large gap between business and IT. It is not uncommon to speak of "alienation."

In the preceding chapters of this book, hypotheses were formulated that have direct consequences for today's IT department and its organizational anchoring. On the one hand, we explained that IT demand and innovation management is managed better in the business units. This decentralized anchoring is advantageous, because a close and constant exchange of information on requirements and business innovations is a central success factor for the future IT function (see chapter "Development and operation are not decisive: IT management follows the "innovate-design-transform" paradigm"). This applies to early planning phases, as well as the subsequent implementation of requirements or business innovations. Furthermore, we explained why it is to be expected that the development of IT solutions and their operations will become less important and can be performed well by external service providers. In this context, public-cloud infrastructures are also perceived as a backbone of future IT landscapes (see chapters "Infrastructure as commodity: IT infrastructure services are traded on free markets and purchased as required" and "Transformable IT landscapes: IT architectures are standardized, modular, flexible, ubiquitous, elastic, cost-effective, and secure").

These developments imply that the central functional components of today's IT departments are no longer needed or—to be more precise—are subject to an outsourcing trend. Assuming that the initiation and implementation of projects and IT operations currently make up approximately 90% of a classic IT department's workforce, the question that arises is how to proceed further and whether a separate IT department makes sense at all in its various, currently prevalent forms (central IT, shared service company, decentralized IT departments, etc.).

Planning, Control, and Coordination Remains

It will not be possible to completely do without an IT function, despite its expected massive reduction. After all, there are a number of tasks that still have to be carried out centrally to ensure efficient and effective IT value creation. First of all, it should be noted that *centralized enterprise architecture management* remains essential. The huge advantages of decentralized processing of demand and innovation management, as well as decentralized implementation of IT projects, are that they have a particular customer proximity and that the IT experts gain ongoing insight into business objectives, strategies, and processes. At the same time, however, it also carries the risk that the various individual activities in the business areas and departments will lead to an increase in the complexity of the IT architecture. This, in turn, can have a negative impact on the cost structure, the quality of service provision, and risks. Central architecture management is therefore necessary. It ensures that the overall architecture is further developed in a targeted manner by means of architectural standards and principles, planning and control processes, as well as architectural governance.

Closely linked to architecture management is *central monitoring of the local demand and innovation management*, as well as a *central project portfolio management*. This is the only way in which to identify and manage the potential synergies and dependencies between local activities in a targeted manner. For example, this prevents similar or identical projects from being carried out simultaneously in different company areas.

Shortening the value chain increases the dependence on external service providers. Digitalization projects can also lead to new technology partnerships and, thus, to further dependencies. It is therefore important that suppliers and partners are systematically selected, and that appropriate strategic relationships are systematically maintained. For this reason, *strategic supplier and provider management* is important, which ensures that all IT-related procurement and cooperation processes follow a uniform strategy and are handled consistently. Conversely, supplier selection and partnership decisions at local level, which are in conflict with decisions taken elsewhere in the company, should be avoided.

The relocation of large parts of the IT value chain does not make *continuous monitoring of project and operational activities* obsolete. In future, IT departments will also not be able to neglect tasks, such as IT controlling, project controlling, and service level management. This will, however, very often involve operational supplier and provider management instead of monitoring and controlling internal processes.

With the increasing dependence on information technology and increasing intervention by the legislative authorities, central risk, compliance, and security management will become more important. The main objective here is to meet legal requirements for IT-based value creation and, in addition, to identify, avoid, or at least reduce, important (security) risks or risks associated with continued business activities. This includes both technical and social/personnel risks. For example, it is essential to protect oneself against technical attacks from outside, to make the IT landscape fail-safe and fault-tolerant, and to avoid safety-related misconduct on the part of employees, or to limit corresponding damage.

In addition to the above-mentioned direct planning and control activities, it is also important to develop a incentive system, which ensures that IT employees (also the decentralized ones) act in accordance with their objectives (IT governance). This also includes the definition of decision-making rights and duties, control and reporting processes, as well as basic rules with regard to IT-related management decisions.

The common denominator of all these tasks is that they do not directly affect IT value creation, they are quite strategic, they require particularly qualified and experienced employees in the majority of cases, and they have a number of interfaces to other corporate functions. For example, there is a link to enterprise controlling, because it involves central control and monitoring processes. The corporate strategy and business development functions are affected, because in times of digitalization, business development and IT innovations can hardly be separated. Operational functions, such as production and logistics, can also be affected, on condition that there are effects of digitalization (we can assume this fundamentally—see chapter "No business without IT: IT is the central and indispensable driver of entrepreneurial value creation").

The question that arises is where such a strategic, small, highly specialized company function can be reasonably anchored in the organization. It is questionable whether it can be fully effective as a department on the second or third management level.

The Development Path from the IT Department to the Executive Portfolio for Digitalization

In fact, initial studies have shown that the requirements stemming from digitalization, the development of decentralized IT functions (for IT demand and innovation management), and the shortening of the IT value chain, suggest an organizational shift in the future IT function. Today's IT functions are organizationally too far away from top decision-makers in order to help shape necessary innovation and digitalization decisions. It is also difficult to carry out central planning and control functions across many business units and functions if the IT department is located two or three levels below the top management level.

Unsurprisingly, companies that are particularly innovative and successful in the context of digitalization are already pursuing other paths and anchoring the tasks outlined above elsewhere in the company. We identified two specific scenarios: (1) In future, the remaining IT function will either be tied, as a staff position, to an existing executive board function, for example the CEO. Already today, this model can be observed in a modified form. However, since most IT functions are not yet as streamlined as described above, only parts, such as IT innovation management and the management of digitalization initiatives, are organized as staff units. (2) As an alternative, the IT function will be transferred to a separate executive board responsibility. In this case, we are already talking about the chief digital officer (CDO)—a function that is not yet particularly widespread. There are only an estimated 1000 such positions worldwide [1]. It is questionable whether the term CDO will become established in the long term. It is less questionable that, in times of digitalization, the IT function must be represented—more than ever before—by an executive board position at top management level. It is conceivable that further tasks are linked to the functions described above, such as the corporate strategy function. This makes sense especially in industries that implement completely digital business models and strategies.

From many IT executives' point of view, the question that arises is how to initiate and advance the transformation towards a new IT function close to the executive board. Presently, the starting points are very different. Basically, we can distinguish between three development stages of today's IT departments: In the first stage, IT can be seen as a *"technical delivery function."* Departments in the first stage focus on the successful execution of IT projects and smooth IT operations. This focus is expressed in a special emphasis on operational functions, such as IT service management or IT project management. IT departments in this stage have, above all, technical and, in most cases, less business know-how.

In the second stage, the IT function is transformed into a *customer-oriented service organization.* Here, it is recognized that the performance of the IT function depends to a large extent on whether business understanding and consulting competence are available and whether there is a partnership with the business functions. This is expressed, for example, in pronounced demand management, which provides many interfaces to IT customers. Business analysts and domain architects have sufficient technical expertise to enable the IT department to transform customer requirements into business solutions.

In the third stage, the IT department becomes the *designer of digital transformation.* Here, companies understand that digital business innovation is only feasible if business and IT functions work together creatively on a long-term basis. This stage is characterized by IT innovation management, or also by co-location concepts. IT specialists do not only understand business requirements and processes; they also understand industry trends, as well as the business potential of IT, and they creatively develop new business models, products, and services in close collaboration with the business areas.

The development of an IT department in the direction of a strategic staff unit, or its own executive board position, is of course easiest if it is at stage three. At stage one, this change is particularly difficult. Here, the IT department is usually seen as a pure service provider. Since more and more business areas are taking independent action with regard to digital innovations, the perception of IT as an innovator is constantly decreasing [2]. In such cases, it is difficult to initiate a new perception among board members, which recognizes that the IT function is crucial for sustainable business success. Frequently, parallel to the existing IT function, units for IT innovation management and digitalization are created, which then have access to top management and can slowly expand their role. In such cases, the traditional IT department will find it difficult to take on the above tasks in the long term. IT departments in stage two have a medium risk of failing to complete the transformation successfully.

What About the CIO?

For today's CIO, the question is how to approach this development. Without proactive action, paradoxically, there is a danger that the person responsible for the foundation of the digital transformation will fall victim to it. There will hardly be any patent remedies—every individual situation is too unique. Today's CIOs, however, will be well advised to take action through various initiatives. On the one hand, they should actively seek a dialog with the top management level. It is important to discuss what digitalization means for the company, how business models, products, and services will change, and what role information technology and the IT department will play in this context. IT managers should prepare well for these discussions. Knowledge of industry developments, competitors' activities, concrete digitalization ideas, and approaches to their implementation, can help them position themselves as a competent advisor in this area. At the same time, IT managers should consistently follow the path towards increased customer and innovation orientation. If they have not yet established a functioning demand and innovation management system, they need to do so. In this context, the consulting and business competencies of the IT staff must be developed further. In individual cases, it can also make sense to enter into coalitions with executives on the business side to initiate and drive joint digitalization initiatives—on the one hand to position themselves appropriately in the organization, and on the other hand to produce success stories. In keeping with the above developments, they should simultaneously prepare the IT architecture for future changes (see chapter "Infrastructure as commodity: IT infrastructure services are traded on free markets and purchased as required").

Overview: The End of the IT Department
- The existence of classic IT departments is in jeopardy, due to the far-reaching reduction of IT value chain depth and close cooperation with the business units.
- The future IT department will primarily assume strategic coordination functions in the context of digital transformation and will work together with almost all business units.
- The tasks of the future IT department will include enterprise architecture management, coordination of demand and innovation management, central portfolio management, strategic supplier and provider management, external monitoring of service provision, risk, compliance and security management, as well as IT governance.
- It is questionable whether anchoring IT departments at the second or third management level is sufficient to fulfill these tasks effectively.
- For this reason, future IT departments will gain their own executive position or become a staff unit of an executive board position.
- Here, they have the necessary proximity to top management.
- CIOs and IT managers should prepare for this development at an early stage and position themselves accordingly.

References

1. Lubkowitz, M. (2015, October 16). Der CDO ist in Deutschland ein seltenes Exemplar. *Internet World Business.* http://www.internetworld.de/technik/digitale-transformation/cdo-in-deutschland-seltenes-exemplar-1034125.html
2. Jeschek, C. (2015, December 8). Talent-Management in der IT: Die klassische IT-Organisation hat ausgedient. *CIO.* http://www.cio.de/a/die-klassische-it-organisation-hat-ausgedient,3251385

Demography, Digital Natives, and Individual Entrepreneurship: Employees Become a Strategic Competitive Factor

In the previous chapters, we described—in detail—the challenges and implications of the digital transformation and outlined our expectations and recommendations regarding the future structure of the IT department. An aspect that has been neglected thus far, is the employee's role in digital change. Exactly as in the past, transformations in the corporate context cannot be mastered without the right and, above all, properly trained employees. However, the trend towards digitalization particularly requires qualifications and skills that are rare in the current labor market. Moreover, the digital working environment is, in many cases, only conditionally compatible with the conservative and hierarchically organized environment of large corporations. Even though the upcoming "war for talents" was forecast and discussed several years ago [1], access to good employees seems to have become a strategic competitive factor at present. More and more "traditional" companies find it difficult to identify new and retain existing employees, especially those with the necessary "digital skills," for example in IT development or data analysis. For many young career starters, large IT companies, such as Google or Microsoft, or the small, dynamic start-ups are more attractive. There are various reasons for the current personnel-related challenges that companies face. In the following, we will get to the bottom of these causes: first with regard to the demographic and labor market development (macro-perspective) and then with regard to the employees' development (micro-perspective).

The Macro Perspective: Demography and Labor Market Trends

The current demographic change is a major reason why recruiting and retaining good employees is an ongoing challenge for many companies. Most western societies are characterized by the fact that, for a couple of decades already, the mortality rate is higher than the birth rate. Despite migration movements, many have a gradual population decline. Due to increasing life expectancy and declining birth rates, the

© Springer International Publishing AG, part of Springer Nature 2019
N. Urbach, F. Ahlemann, *IT Management in the Digital Age*, Management for Professionals, https://doi.org/10.1007/978-3-319-96187-3_12

share of older people in relation to the share of younger people is rising. For instance, the German population pyramid has deformed accordingly. In continuously growing countries, the lower age groups are strongly represented, while the upper age groups are gradually decreasing—similar to a pyramid tapering from bottom to top. In Germany, the distribution has changed in recent decades. The baby boomers of the mid-sixties have become older and have, thus, moved up in the statistics, followed by younger, age groups that are smaller as a result of the birth decline. Accordingly, the pyramid turned into an urn or, to put it more nicely, into a Christmas tree [2].

The effects of demographic change present new challenges for society. For the economy—at least for the domestic market—this development has resulted not only in falling demand and a change in customer segments, but—above all—in a shrinking labor market. Although the size of the total population is declining comparatively slowly, the working age population, and thus the available labor force potential, is declining much faster. In 2011, the Federal Ministry of the Interior in Germany published a demographic report showing that, under the given circumstances, the number of employed persons in Germany is likely to decline by up to 50% by 2050, compared to the year 2000 [3]. The availability of increasingly fewer well-qualified young workers is a consequence of this development. There is, however, a trend towards an increasingly older workforce—usually with good mental and physical fitness. Companies, therefore, need to be an attractive employer to young workers, but they also need to include older employers in "modern knowledge work."

In addition to the general shortage of skilled workers, the unsatisfied demand for STEM experts is likely to become a greater challenge for many companies in light of the specific demands on employees in the field of digitalization. The term STEM refers to the combination of subjects or professions in the fields of science, technology, engineering, and mathematics. For the past few years, the labor market in the STEM sector has been attracting a great deal of attention. On the one hand, this is due to the fact that STEM occupations are regarded as key drivers of economic innovation. Considering Western industries in terms of their innovative results and skilled workforce, it becomes clear that STEM qualifications and innovative strength are closely correlated. On the other hand, the STEM labor market is also much discussed, because of a larger training and manpower gap in this area—with a simultaneous increase in demand for STEM employees. Recent studies have come to the conclusion that, without additional measures to secure skilled workers, a shortfall of approximately 670,000 STEM experts in Germany alone is expected by 2020—only to meet current demand. If the expected future demand is taken into account, the gap will increase even further [4]. Publicly, as well as privately, funded projects and initiatives have emerged to increase the supply of skilled workers in this sector in view of early forecasts that a shortage of skilled workers is to be expected in this area. Despite these efforts, however, it is likely that well-trained employees with the skills relevant for digital transformation will continue to be a scarce commodity in future.

The trend towards declining numbers of well-trained skilled workers is countered by a rising demand for such workers. The reason for this development is that knowledge work is generally more central in many successful companies. Due to the change from the industrial to the information age, knowledge work is becoming increasingly important, especially in highly developed national economies. Accordingly, corporate value creation focuses much stronger on individual employees than only a few years ago [5]. Successful knowledge work, which requires highly trained employees, enables the development and production of innovative products and services. Ultimately, it leads to sustainable competitive advantages. The employee required for this is creative, innovative, works in networks and teams, moves internationally, and is flexible. For modern companies, the results that employees achieve are much more important than the hours that they work. An entrepreneur expresses the current situation as follows: "My most important asset has feet. Every evening it leaves the company. I can only hope that it will come back the next morning" [6].

The Micro-Perspective: The IT Employee Yesterday and Today

In addition to considering demographic developments and changes in the labor market, a change is also noticeable at the micro level—among the employees themselves. This change is mainly driven by the changed value system of many succeeding employees, which, compared to previous generations of employees, is very strongly influenced by a desire for individuality and self-determination [7]. Despite the employee's role, many employees of the younger generations are looking for individual entrepreneurship within their own company ("corporate entrepreneurship") [8]. Changes in typical work histories also play a major role. While previous generations of employees often committed to a single employer at an early stage and for a long time, the working life of today's generation of knowledge workers is very often characterized by a frequent change of employer and career reorientations [9]. These changes have consequence for companies in that it is harder to bind employees to the company. What particularly young employees expect and demand in their jobs, has changed, too. Only a few years ago, financial incentives and good career prospects were the main criteria for selecting an employer; at present, these can increasingly be understood as hygiene factors. Topics such as work–life balance, compatibility of work and family life, as well as a good working environment and equipment, come into the foreground when selecting and making decisions [10].

In addition to these general changes on the employee side, the IT labor market plays a special role in the digitalization area. In order to illustrate the specific challenges to which companies must respond, we need to investigate the changes in this specific area in recent years. Only a few years ago, the IT labor market was essentially a buyer's market. Although it was already difficult to acquire the necessary skills in certain specific areas (e.g., for specific programming languages), companies were generally able to recruit the necessary IT staff on the labor market at more or less manageable costs. Furthermore, the typical work histories remained predominantly constant. It was not unusual for an employee to have worked for only one or a few employers during his or her working life. In the past, there have also been constant technological developments, but many qualifications could be used over comparatively long periods of time. The majority of the further developments were incremental and could be addressed via corresponding training and further education. At the same time, the labor market was relatively well supplied with graduates. The classic IT-related study courses, such as computer science and information systems, were perceived as quite attractive and therefore in demand. In addition to general virtues, such as conscientiousness and reliability, the main focus in recruiting was—above all—on the hard skills, that is, usually the employee's specific technical know-how in the desired domain. The attractiveness of the job could then be ensured—quite simply—through attractive remuneration and sufficient career opportunities.

In recent years, the IT labor market has changed dramatically and developed into a seller's market. The gap between the supply and demand of qualified IT workers has widened accordingly. At the same time, the work histories of many employees have become much more diverse. For the employer, this means that employees change employers more frequently and in a comparatively quick succession. Therefore, they remain in the company for a shorter period of time. The new tasks arising from digital transformation also require very specific—and therefore rare—employee skills. In chapter "Development and operation are not decisive: IT management follows the "innovate-design-transform" paradigm" we have already dealt with the changes in the required organizational capabilities of the future IT department. In order to implement these skills, however, appropriate employees with the necessary compe- tence profiles are also required. For example, the American market research com- pany, Forrester, identifies eight employee roles that should exist in the IT department during the digitalization era: relationship managers, architects, project and program managers, vendor managers, user experience experts, data experts, business process designers, and security experts [11]. Regardless of whether exactly these eight employee roles are decisive, we agree with the assessment that both the breadth of competence profiles within the IT department, as well as the depth of IT competencies within the business units, will increase. In addition, qualities such as entrepreneurial thinking and acting, creativity, agility and innovation ability, as well as a general affinity for digital technologies will be required. The ever-shorter innovation cycles are gradually reducing the half-life of qualifications and skills. As a result, digitaliza- tion constantly requires new qualifications. At the same time, we have noticed a relatively low demand for IT and information systems university programs in recent years. This, in our view, is less due to the programs offered than to the perceived attractiveness of the classic IT occupations. It is very slowly dawning on first-year students that a solid (basic) education in IT-related subjects is an essential basis for a large proportion of current and, above all, future careers.

Current Developments Have a Massive Impact on Attracting and Retaining Good IT Staff

The current demographic development, the resulting labor market situation in general and the STEM sector in particular, as well as the changes in IT employees themselves, have resulted in a significant challenge for many companies to recruit and retain well-trained IT staff. Although this is likely to affect all business sizes and sectors, at least in the long term, small and medium-sized enterprises, as well as companies outside large cities and metropolitan areas, are likely to face particularly big challenges. This is mainly due to the fact that large companies are generally better known and often perceived as more attractive. Due to the trend of recent years towards living in large cities and centers, the rural regions are usually even more under supplied in terms of young, well-trained employees.

In 2013, a study by Capgemini Consulting concludes that the "war for talents" has become a digital war [12]. The authors of the study expect that, in the coming years, 90% of all occupations will require information and communication technology skills and that big data alone will create a global need for more than four million new jobs of which only a third are likely to be filled. Although companies are very much aware of this gap and its importance, there is hardly any investment in the training and further education of digital skills. Improvement potential is perceived—above all else—as part of human resource (HR) management, which—according to the study—rarely uses innovative staff recruitment methods and has a very passive approach to the topic of competence development.

The consequence of the above-described "digital skills gap" can be summarized quite simply for the digital company. Recruiting and retaining employees is becoming a central success factor for the company. And not only that. In our view, recruiting and retaining good employees is no longer merely a specific functional task that can only be performed by the HR department. This is, instead, a challenge that concerns the entire company. In addition to traditional HR management, the necessary activities also relate to corporate culture, workplace design and management, as well as business development, which we will discuss in more detail below.

Developing HR Management

The ability to understand and address the challenges of digitalization in terms of recruiting and retaining the necessary employees, is a key task facing traditional HR management. This includes identifying the skills and experience that are really needed in the IT area. In principle, it can be assumed that the requirements for IT employees will change. Interface competence will become even more important than it already is today. Since we presume that the boundaries between a company's business units and IT department are becoming increasingly blurred (see chapter "Shadow IT as a lived practice: IT innovations are developed in interdisciplinary teams within the business departments"), it will be more important for IT staff to be proficient not only in technical terminology, but also in business. In future, pure technicians will, however, be less in demand. Within the digitalization context, the main focus is on identifying, conceptualizing, and designing innovative, IT-based solutions with immediate business benefits. The technical implementation of these solutions can then usually be easily entrusted to a service provider (see chapter "Development and operation are not decisive: IT management follows the "innovate-design-transform" paradigm"). We also expect that role specialization, which we have observed very strongly in recent years, will continue to increase in future.

In this context, HR management need to acknowledge that, in general, it is no longer possible to obtain "fully trained" employees from the graduate market for the specific IT career profiles, due to the generic nature of the courses offered by universities in their Bachelor's and Master's programs. In recent years, the academic landscape has already responded to this development with numerous specialized study courses and degrees; but we are of the opinion that a solid basic training at the interface between business and IT is still very goal-oriented at this stage. At the same time, however, it must be the companies' task to fill the "digital skills gap" by means of "training on the job" and further in-house training initiatives. In order to fill possible resource and competence gaps, close cooperation with knowledge and training partners (e.g., universities and non-university research institutions) can be a promising solution here. Conceivably, a separate function for the development and procurement of IT personnel can be set up if the company-wide human resource (HR) functions are not able to cover the demand in the current setup.

Corporate Culture, Workplace Design, and Management

In addition to advanced HR management, successful companies must position themselves in the digital age as an attractive employer. A task that HR management can initiate and control, but which the entire company and also its management must practice, is creating a corporate culture that is perceived as attractive. In this context, it is particularly important to respond to the changed value system of the above-mentioned young generations of employees. Here, important adjustments can be the creation of an attractive working environment and modern workplace concepts, as well as a modern and target-group-oriented management style.

Creating an attractive working environment can be supported through both the work model and the workplace. The task of corporate leaders is to identify which of the outlined, personnel-related challenges apply to their own company and to what extent they should address them through developing the knowledge workplace further. The development of modern work concepts is more associated with location-independent work, distributed work beyond time zones, changes of private and professional phases, as well as non-regulated working hours [13]. Furthermore, it is important to offer employees specific benefits that support a work–life balance in the best possible way. These include childcare, as well as sports and fitness facilities. Specific training and further education programs do not only offer benefits for the company; they are often also attractive to individual employees, since they can broaden their professional horizons and increase their market value.

The physical workplace design equipped with modern information technology plays a very important role. The main aim here is to create an attractive environment in which employees enjoy working and in which innovations can be born. Against the background of increasingly distributed working, it is particularly important to create dedicated spaces in which people can meet and in which they can work creatively. Furthermore, a high degree of self-determination in the employees' workflows is particularly important. Accordingly, the employee must be given a free choice of methods and provided with the corresponding software. Different devices (own and company hardware) should be supported as working tools, which will depend on the working context. Here, it should be noted that the tolerance for poor usability, especially among users of the "digital natives" generation, is becoming ever smaller, which naturally also applies to the company's own employees (see chapter "Focusing on the user: development processes are agile, end-user-centered, and merged with the operation"). Developing the knowledge workplace further has many implications for IT management. At the core of the necessary change, is a changed organizational and IT architecture into which the "knowledge workplace of the future" must be integrated [12].

In view of the current changes in the digitalization era, the question that arises is whether the established "analog" business management concepts can still be justified and are up-to-date. We believe that the changed value system of the next employee generations requires a specific management culture. The detailed characteristics of such future management concepts are currently discussed—very intensively—under the "Leadership 4.0" keyword. Even if, as expected, there is no consensus on the design of modern management concepts, there is nevertheless a largely unanimous opinion that hierarchical systems in the classic form have had their day. In future, managers with good communication skills, and who have a sensitive and trusting relationship with their employees, will be much more successful [14]. A study commissioned by the German Federal Ministry of Labor and Social Affairs examined the "changing management culture" and conducted 400 in-depth interviews with managers. As a core result, it presents ten requirements that modern managers must meet at present and in future. This includes, amongst others, enabling flexibility and diversity, an ability to professionally design open-ended processes, an ability to cooperate and motivate through self-determination and appreciation [15] Also with regard to their management culture, companies are called upon to question their current positioning and to check whether they fit into the digital world.

Google (or Alphabet) could serve as a role model for other companies. The Internet company has succeeded in positioning itself as the world's most popular employer among students of both technical and business management study courses [16]. It may be worthwhile for companies to take a closer look at what Google, as an attractive employer, has to offer its potential and existing employees. The company undoubtedly benefits from its brand image and employee remuneration is also a major contributor. However, Google has also managed to create very pleasant working conditions, which are not at the expense of productivity and innovation. These include attractive workplace design and equipment, free meals, shuttle buses, wellness areas, and fitness training. The employees are, thus, offered numerous options that simply increase the fun factor when working. Other factors include relatively flat hierarchies, a high degree of self-determination in work design, as well as freedom for innovation work. For example, the working hours model, which exempts employees from regular working hours 1 day a week, has resulted in a number of innovative services. Through these various measures, Google has succeeded in blurring the boundaries between leisure and work while, at the same time, creating an innovative working atmosphere.

Business Development: Gaining IT Skills Through Site Selection, Acquisitions, and Cooperation

Many companies are currently experiencing—with regret—that the acquisition of IT skills can no longer be achieved by classic personnel recruitment and development alone. In order to be successful in this area, a more far-reaching perspective is required, which includes a targeted choice of location, competence-enhancing acquisitions, and strategic cooperation.

Choosing the right location is becoming more important for firms. The willingness to move and to leave the familiar social environment is declining among many, especially young, working people. Today's employee is, therefore, considered less flexible than a few years ago. If today's young workers still accept a relocation, it is increasingly relevant to their decisions that the new center of their lives will also be attractive outside the working environment. Here, aspects such as recreational value, transport connections, cultural offerings, the general quality of life, and nature all play a role. Last but not least, the location also determines the labor supply. There are regions where it is traditionally more difficult to find highly qualified IT personnel than is the case in the large metropolitan areas and/or around universities.

However, modern HR management and a successful choice of location are not always sufficient to cover your own IT personnel requirements. Therefore, an increasing number of companies are considering—in order to compensate for their competence deficits—targeted acquisitions of other companies (often software companies). Such acquisitions have obvious advantages. The buying company gains access to know-how, new product innovations, and—finally—to appropriately trained personnel in the shortest possible time. There are, however, also disadvantages and risks to be considered in such an approach. These include, above all else, the customary high price, the often difficult to reconcile corporate cultures, as well as the fluctuation of employees associated with an acquisition. Strategic cooperation could therefore be a middle way. The goal is to compensate for competence deficits by cooperating closely with companies that have the necessary skills. The cooperating companies can, for example, develop and market new products and services together (see chapter "Innovations through networks: turning strategic suppliers into innovation partners").

Strong Competition Requires Quick Action

These personnel-related challenges also raise the question of how corporate leaders should respond and how the transformation from the old to the new world should be shaped. At this stage, we recommend that companies tackle the necessary change as quickly and consistently as possible. We assume that future corporate success depends—more than ever—on the constant availability of the brightest minds. True to the motto "birds of a feather flock together," successful companies will find it much easier to retain the best employees. Companies that do not manage to retain the employees required for digital transformation, will not produce the necessary innovations to survive in the increasingly dynamic competition of the future. Once lost, it will be extremely difficult to get back on the road to success.

Overview: Demography, Digital Natives, and Individual Entrepreneurship
- Due to demographic change, the labor market has fewer and fewer well-trained staff at its disposal.
- In particular, the unsatisfied demand for STEM experts is becoming a greater challenge for many companies.
- Digital transformation requires specific qualifications and skills of IT staff, which are correspondingly scarce in the current labor market.
- In addition, compared to previous generations, the new employee generations, have a changed value system and a desire for individual entrepreneurship.
- Recruiting and retaining well-trained IT staff has already become a significant challenge for many companies.
- In response to the digital skills gap, changes are needed in HR management, corporate culture, workplace design, leadership, as well as business development.
- Companies should tackle personnel challenges in a timely manner, since having the right people on board, has become a strategic competitive factor.

References

1. Chambers, E., Foulon, M., Handfield-Jones, H., Hankin, S., & Michaels, E. (1998). The war for talent. *The McKinsey Quarterly, 3*, 44–57.
2. Elmer, C., & Schäfer, M. (2015, April 5). Wie die Pyramide zum Weihnachtsbaum wird. *Spiegel Online*. http://www.spiegel.de/wissenschaft/mensch/demografischer-wandel-pyramide-wird-zum-weihnachtsbaum-a-1026684.html
3. Bundesministerium des Innern. (2011, October). *Demografiebericht – Bericht der Bundesregierung zur demografischen Lage und künftigen Entwicklung des Landes*. http://www.bmi.bund.de/DE/Themen/Gesellschaft-Verfassung/Demografie/Demografiebericht/demografiebericht_node.html

4. Institut der deutschen Wirtschaft Köln. (2015, May 18). *MINT-Frühjahrsreport 2015, MINT – Regionale Stärken und Herausforderungen, Gutachten für BDA, BDI, MINT Zukunft schaffen und Gesamtmetall.* http://www.arbeitgeber.de/www%5Carbeitgeber.nsf/res/MINT-Fruehjahrsreport_2015.pdf/$file/MINT-Fruehjahrsreport_2015.pdf

5. Dörhöfer, S. (2012). *Management und Organisation von Wissensarbeit: Strategie, Arbeitssystem und organisationale Praktiken in wissensbasierten Unternehmen.* Wiesbaden: VS Verlag für Sozialwissenschaften.

6. IPCH. (2008). *Entmystifizierung der Produktivität. Vom Kernbegriff Produktivität zur Wissensproduktivität.* White Paper des Schweizerischen Produktivitätsinstituts AG. https://static1.squarespace.com/static/5109428de4b04ea0ec18ef88/t/52456273e4b0dedb521bd7f7/1380278899625/Entmystifizierung+der+Produktivitt.pdf

7. Kurzmann, S. (2015). *Individualität und Flexibilität im Personalmanagement: Die neue Herausforderung durch die Generation Y.* Hamburg: Diplomica Verlag.

8. Kühn, C., Eymann, T., Urbach, N., & Schweizer, A. (2016). From professionals to entrepreneurs – HR practices as an enabler for fostering corporate entrepreneurship in professional service firms. *German Journal of Research in Human Resource Management, 30*(2), 125–154.

9. Nawatzki, J. (2013). *Mit Selbstcoaching zum Traumjob: Wie Sie in fünf Schritten Ihre wahre Berufung entdecken und umsetzen.* Wiesbaden: Springer Fachmedien.

10. Stepstone. (2011). StepStone employer branding report 2011. http://www.stepstone.de/Ueber-StepStone/upload/StepStone_Employer_Branding_Report_2011_final.pdf

11. Pütter, C. (2015, September 9). Mitarbeiter-Rollen: 8 notwendige IT-Skills für die Digitalisierung. *Computerwoche.* http://www.computerwoche.de/a/8-notwendige-it-skills-fuer-die-digitalisierung,3090227

12. Capgemini Consulting. (2013). The digital talent gap: Developing skills for today's digital organizations. https://www.capgemini.com/resource-file-access/resource/pdf/the_digital_talent_gap27-09_0.pdf

13. Urbach, N., & Ahlemann, F. (2016). Der Wissensarbeitsplatz der Zukunft: Trends, Herausforderungen und Implikationen für das strategische IT-Management. *HMD – Praxis der Wirtschaftsinformatik, 53*(1), 16–28.

14. Fendt, U. (2015, Oktober 23). Führung im Zeitalter der Digitalisierung. *Computerwoche.* http://www.computerwoche.de/a/fuehrung-im-zeitalter-der-digitalisierung,3217788

15. Initiative Neue Qualität der Arbeit. (2014, September 2014). *Führungskultur im Wandel.* http://www.inqa.de/DE/Angebote/Publikationen/fuehrungskultur-im-wandel-monitor.html;jsessionid=13607F25509C3C463A479A18BF5C215E

16. Dämon, K. (2015, June 24). Alle lieben Google – Die beliebtesten Arbeitgeber der Welt. *WirtschaftsWoche.* http://www.wiwo.de/erfolg/campus-mba/alle-lieben-google-die-besten-arbeitgeber-der-welt/11930316.html

Summary and Conclusion

In this book we analyzed the current trend of digitalization. We presented and explained ten hypotheses on the development of IT management, as well as the IT department in companies. Digitalization as a trend is unstoppable and will change many companies significantly. This will lead to new products, services, as well as value creation and business models that we are currently unable to imagine. The effects of intelligent systems that use sensors to perceive the environment, learn independently, and analyze unimaginable amounts of data in the shortest possible time may perhaps be even less conceivable. We must not imagine such systems as only isolated computer system. The special potential of digitalization is that computers interact in a global network. Current IT departments are massively affected by these developments. It is very questionable whether their current organizational anchors, task portfolios, depth of value creation, cultures, and their current cooperation with other business units are suitable for keeping pace with digitalization and taking on a shaping role. Those who do not want to become obsolete by these developments should be vigilant and closely observe current trends, as well as technological innovations. But that by itself will not be sufficient. Structures, processes, partnerships, and also the company culture must be prepared in such a way that rapid, agile action and reaction is possible when business opportunities arise from digitalization or when technologies have attained the necessary maturity. In detail, IT managers can—already at present—take a number of measures to position themselves. These include, for example, the optimization of the IT architecture and its preparation with regard to the use of public cloud services, intensified cooperation with the business units, and the establishment of technology scouting. Successful digitalization projects can be used as success stories to position themselves as competent partners.

The meaning of our hypotheses should not be misunderstood. They can either be realized as described or they can be realized in another form. Their function is to inspire, spark discussion, and align their plans. The future scenarios described in the previous chapters are deliberately not dated. It is impossible to state without any

© Springer International Publishing AG, part of Springer Nature 2019   119
N. Urbach, F. Ahlemann, *IT Management in the Digital Age*, Management for
Professionals, https://doi.org/10.1007/978-3-319-96187-3_13

doubt which company and which industry, as well as when and how, are affected by digitalization. For certain industries, for example, it is possible to say that the first waves of digitalization have already been completed, for example in the areas of music, newspapers, and retail. Other industries are currently undergoing a major wave of digitalization, such as mechanical engineering (Industry 4.0). In other sectors no major disruptive changes are to be expected, at least in the short to medium term, for example in parts of the chemical industry. Digitalization will also not be a once-off process, as some publications like to suggest. There will always be new technologies with disruptive potential. Maybe even more often. Often it only needs incremental developments to enable a technology to fully exploit its potential. The music industry has been revolutionized several times in this way. After the spread of MP3 technology combined with corresponding distribution channels (for example Apple iTunes) in the last decade, we are currently experiencing the next revolution by establishing streaming services such as Spotify or Deezer. Digitalization's special characteristic is that it is progressing very quickly. In many cases, this can be explained through network effects. New business models tend to develop sluggishly over a longer period of time, until user numbers accelerate considerably, with almost exponential growth. Then, the figures generally stabilize at a high level (at least for market-leading companies). We are accustomed to see these phenomena for consumer technologies. But we will probably see that such waves can also be realized for business technologies. The Industry 4.0 concept with networked machines, especially in the inter-organizational area, only makes sense if as many companies as possible use corresponding technologies based on open standards. That is why we encourage executives to be very vigilant in order to prevent their companies from becoming like Kodak—once the world leader in photo film technology, but overslept the transition to digital photography and now only has a shadow existence. Kodak was caught cold; contrary to all predictions, the digital photography business exploded in such a short time and analog photography virtually disappeared in the same short time that any attempts to keep up were hopeless. The product development cycles were too long compared to the dynamic market development. The motto can thus only be: Start today to be successful tomorrow. It is important for companies to avoid being demoted and robbed of their competitive position by established competitors, as well as small startups.

Appendix

CPSIA information can be obtained
at www.ICGtesting.com
Printed in the USA
LVHW011807041118
595903LV00012B/683/P